Candidly, Allen Funt

Candidly, Allen Funt

A Million Smiles Later

ALLEN FUNT

WITH PHILIP REED

BARRICADE BOOKS INC. / New York

Published by Barricade Books Inc.
61 Fourth Avenue
New York, NY 10003

Printed in the United States of America

Funt, Allen, 1914-
       Candidly, Allen Funt / by Allen Funt.
              p. cm.
       ISBN 1-56980-008-1: $22.00
       1. Funt, Allen, 1914-   . 2. Television personalities—United States—Biography. 3. Candid camera (Television program) I. Title.
PN1992.4.F86A3 1994
791.45'028'092—dc20
[B]   93-44936
                                           CIP

First Printing

D E D I C A T I O N

There are many longtime friends and associates who have helped me during my career. There are newer acquaintances to whom I am grateful for their help with this book. But I dedicate this particular project to the eight people who have given me support and love throughout my life.

My five children: Peter, who has the unenviable challenge of following in his dad's footsteps; Patricia, an antiques dealer by profession and a sweetheart by nature; John, a gifted artist and successful events planner, and Juliet and William, who came late, caught up quickly, and are seeking their fortunes as actors. And the women who have put up with me: Evelyn, Marilyn, and Anne.—A.F.

C O N T E N T S

CHAPTER ONE: The Boomerang Effect 9

SIDEBAR: The Real Me? 21

CHAPTER TWO: Into Hiding 23

SIDEBAR: What's in a Name? 39

CHAPTER THREE: "Candid Camera" Is Born 41

SIDEBAR: Candid Persuaders 59

CHAPTER FOUR: Entering the Golden Age 63

SIDEBAR: Censored! Censored! 73

CHAPTER FIVE: A Day With "Candid Camera" 75

SIDEBAR: Pure Inspiration 87

CHAPTER SIX: Affairs of Art and Heart 89

SIDEBAR: Keep on Smiling 99

CHAPTER SEVEN: Cast and Characters 101

SIDEBAR: The Art of Listening 117

CHAPTER EIGHT: Candid Kids 119

SIDEBAR: Man vs. Machine 131

CHAPTER NINE: All the World's a Stage 133

SIDEBAR: Candid Categories 143

CHAPTER TEN: The Cleanest "Dirty" Movie 145

SIDEBAR: No Release 159

CHAPTER ELEVEN: Money Talks 161

SIDEBAR: A Form for Every Format 173

CHAPTER TWELVE: Moving West 175

SIDEBAR: A Web of Words 187

CHAPTER THIRTEEN: Rip-Offs, Spin-Offs, and Specials 189

SIDEBAR: Types of Reactions 201

CHAPTER FOURTEEN: The Top Ten 203

SIDEBAR: Famous Faces 217

CHAPTER FIFTEEN: Laughing Matters 219

EPILOGUE 231

The Boomerang Effect

We were about an hour out of Newark when I heard a terrible commotion in the back of the jet. I turned and saw a man dragging the flight attendant up the aisle, holding a butcher knife to her throat. He walked her the whole length of the jet, disappeared into the cockpit, and slammed the door. Everyone on the plane was frozen with fear. A few minutes later, the captain got on the intercom and confirmed what we already suspected—we had been skyjacked and were going to Cuba.

It was 1969 and I was with my wife, Marilyn; our babies, Juliet and William; a nurse; and three members of my film crew. We were flying to Miami to film "Candid Camera" and a sequence for my feature-length movie *What Do You Say to a Naked Lady?*

I turned to my wife to reassure her. But before I could speak, she said, "It's your fault. You had to fly out of Newark, didn't you?"

She was right, of course. It was my fault. We had planned to fly out of JFK, but everything was booked. So we jumped in three cabs and hurried over to Newark—only to have this happen.

But I knew that her accusation held a deeper meaning. What she meant was that it was always my fault when anything went wrong for anyone. Indeed, as the creator and producer of "Candid Camera," it was my business to make things go wrong in people's lives. I had, in a way, become America's provocateur.

I looked up the aisle toward the cockpit, hoping to see what was developing, but my view was blocked by a rather stout woman. Her eyes bore into me accusingly, and she took a threatening step my way.

"Say something," she said. I couldn't figure out what she wanted. So I told her, "Lady I'm as scared as you are. Please don't do anything crazy. Just sit down and leave me alone."

"You've said enough," she barked, and turning to the rest of the plane announced, "Ladies and gentlemen, I'm pleased to tell you this is not a skyjacking. This joker is Allen Funt, and we're all on 'Candid Camera.'"

The plane went absolutely crazy. People began cheering and stamping their feet—with relief, really. The commotion went on for so long and was so loud that the skyjacker stuck his head out of the cabin. This only made matters worse because 150 people gave him a big round of applause.

I slumped down in my seat, trying to disappear. All I could think was that someone would go up to the skyjacker and his partner to congratulate them on their acting performances, and the blood would start to flow.

Looking around, I spotted a priest in the back of the jet. I went over to him and said, "Father, I have no right to ask you for a favor, but maybe they'll believe you. Tell them this is no joke. This maniac is for real."

He studied me for a long time, then smiled and poked me in the ribs. "Oh no you don't," he said. "You're not catching me too." My credibility was shot, even with a man of the cloth. I gave up and returned to my seat.

Luckily, we landed in Cuba before anyone got hurt. Police and soldiers rushed aboard and took the skyjackers away. In those days Cuba was making a lot of money from skyjackings, so we were treated royally. They showered us with cigars and books about Castro. But the passengers were still furious with me. They still thought—even with the soldiers and the Cuban officials—it was a "Candid Camera" gag. They just couldn't get it through their heads that it wasn't "all my fault."

That evening we flew to Miami. After we landed, and everyone filed past me on their way off the plane, they all cursed me in their own unique ways. The last guy stared at me for a long time, then said with a sneer, "Smile, my ass."

Even though it had happened before, this was the first time I clearly identified the "Boomerang Effect" in my life. The Boomerang Effect occurs when the practical joker becomes the butt of life's own jokes. For the past twenty-two years, I had been playing jokes on other people—first on the radio show "Candid Microphone" and later on "Candid Camera." In every conceivable way, we tried to rewrite the script of everyday living to test people's responses. From mailboxes that talked, to cars that split in two, to bowling pins that fell down without being hit, we put ordinary people on the spot.

With the skyjacking, I saw quite clearly how ironic it was that I was perceived as America's number-one practical joker.

I've never been the life of the party. In fact, I haven't worn a single lampshade, danced on a table, or slipped a whoopee cushion under anyone. I was a sensitive kid. I wanted to be an artist. I even went to art school. All along, though, the invisible threads of life were weaving a different pattern for me.

I often wish I could isolate and review each event in my life that led me to "Candid Camera" and beyond into spin-offs, feature films, and, more recently, the study of "Laughter Therapy." Perhaps, somewhere among the many stories I've accumulated, I might find out how it all began. But life is too subtle for such a cause-and-effect analysis. So I'll just tell the stories.

After all, what really matters is that I've had a rare opportunity to study and interact with people in a unique and wonderful way. I've worked with the great actors and athletes and celebrities of our time. I've even come face to face with world leaders and played tricks on our presidents. Most valuable, though, are the laughs I've shared with millions of ordinary men and women—and especially children—who were remarkably good sports when I told them, "Smile! You're on 'Candid Camera.'"

* * * * *

It's many years earlier now. I'm about twelve years old, and I'm standing on a stage in summer camp performing in a play. What's about to happen is one of the few things that foreshadowed the career I was to later pursue. The audience of parents and camp counselors is trying to stay awake for a rather tortured rendition of Eugene O'Neill's *The Emperor Jones*. The stage is decorated to look like the jungle and, on the armrests of the emperor's throne, are cans of burning Sterno that are supposed to look like torches.

Suddenly, in my acting zeal, I overgesture and knock one of the Sterno cans flying. The flaming liquid coats my arm and continues burning! But in a flash, so to speak, I realize that it's the liquid that is burning and not my flesh. So I keep acting. Everyone seems riveted, and they give me a huge round of applause.

That incident taught me two important things that I later used on "Candid Camera": find a way to make use of your mistakes, and always stay in character—no matter what happens.

Other than that incident, there were few clues in my early years that would point to a life spent entertaining audiences with the unexpected. Neither of my parents was in show business. My father, Isidore, had actually studied to be a rabbi. However, somewhere along the line, he became disillusioned with organized religion, although he remained an avid reader and fancied himself a scholar.

My father was born in Russia and, as a young man, worked as a hat salesman. He met my mother, Paula, in a nearby town in Poland, and they were married when my mother was only sixteen. They moved to Belgium and then to the United States, passing through Ellis Island in 1913.

Like many salesmen, my father collected jokes and stories, and he had a great talent for making a small amount of material go a long way. He had perhaps only a dozen stories, but he had the uncanny knack of being able to apply them to any situation.

One story I remember particularly well was about the "village idiot" from my father's town in Russia. The guy runs up to another man and says, "I think I have the problems of the whole world solved. What we do is get the rich to give half their money to the poor." The other man says, "You're crazy, that'll never work." The idiot says, "Don't laugh. I have it half finished already. I've checked with the poor, and they're willing." You can't imagine how many times my father could work that phrase into a conversation: "I checked with the poor, and they're willing."

Before immigrating to this country, my father became a diamond dealer, but once in New York, he found the business had many ups and downs. One year we would have enough money to vacation in Europe; the next we could barely keep the bill collectors at bay. Because of this, perhaps, my father got himself involved in a scheme in which the stewards on ocean liners would bring diamonds into the country to avoid import duties, and dealers such as my father would sell them.

One particular steward named Jimmy was caught and lost his job. He then began pestering my father for handouts, and it continued for several years. This was painful for my father because, in every other way, he was a completely moral man. I can remember that when the phone would ring and it was Jimmy, it sent a chill through our household.

Unlike my father, my mother was anything but a scholar. I don't believe she even finished high school. But what she lacked in education, she made up for with enthusiasm and charm. She loved life, every minute of it. Whenever things were at their worst—and they often were when I was growing up— my mother would always say, "Let's have a party!"

Throughout my childhood, my mother was always involved in raising money for charities. And she was the nerviest person you could ever meet. She would ask anybody for money, but she always bothered them with a great deal of charm. She was a complete optimist and an inspiration to us all.

I was born in Brooklyn, New York, on September 16, 1914. My early days were spent in an apartment on Flatbush Avenue in a modest neighborhood of immigrants and working-class people. My older sister Dorothy had a tremendous impact on my life. Not only was she brilliant, and graduated with every honor known to the world of academics, but she was also pretty. And if that wasn't bad enough, everyone adored her. In short, I hated her.

Once, at age thirteen, my frustration built to the point where one day I couldn't stand her anymore. I don't remember what provoked me, but I picked her up and threw her—fully clothed—into a bathtub full of water. But she was so well-behaved, she didn't fight back. She just scolded me, and that was the end of it—which was more infuriating than anything.

Dorothy became a successful businesswoman and reached the top of a company that dealt with organized labor and union benefits. She was also very radical in her politics, and my father and I would have terrific fights with her. But in the fighting, we saw firsthand how her debating skills paid off in labor management.

In my early days, I knew more about what I *didn't* want to be than what I *did* want to be. I didn't want to be like my sister, and I definitely didn't want to be a diamond dealer. My most vivid memories of the diamond trade are the hours spent on my hands and knees, searching the floor for diamonds my father had dropped—sort of like hunting for a contact lens, only harder.

I had vague dreams of being an athlete, even though I had only average abilities. The test of your talent is how quickly you are picked for a team by your schoolmates. I was always chosen somewhere in the middle—not the last, but never the first. But when we played punchball or football, what I lacked in ability, I made up for with a dogged tenacity.

The only sport I excelled at was boxing. This was thrust on me, to some degree, because my mother insisted on dressing me in black satin shorts with big white pearl buttons down the side. If you were a little Jewish guy dressed like that, and you lived in an Italian neighborhood, you had to know how to take care of yourself. I boxed a lot at summer camp, an upper-class camp where the kids were kind of soft, so I was actually known as being pretty tough.

Self defense was handy at times when I was confronted with anti-Semitism, but the kids in my Brooklyn neighborhood were very fair-minded—they hated anything they were not. So I quickly learned not to take their remarks personally. Probably because of my father's suspicion of organized religion, I didn't have a strong Jewish identity. At one point I remember getting in a conversation with some kids about religion. Finally, I ran over and stood below our apartment window and called up, "Hey Mom! What are we?"

Because of the example that my sister Dorothy set for me, I did fairly well in school. She made me desperate to succeed—at anything. As a result of my good marks, I became the victim of a terrible system where they kept making me skip grades. I graduated from New Utrecht High School at the age of fifteen, studied pictorial illustration at Pratt Institute for a year, then went to Cornell University.

My sister had gone to Cornell (on a triple scholarship, of course), and I found myself in her shadow again. I was too young to be in college, and I was a moody out-of-place guy. My sister got me a job waiting tables in a sorority house that she had been the head of. It was an awful job. We didn't get paid— we just got free meals. That wouldn't have been so bad, except the girls were always on diets and eating things like prune whip, cottage cheese, and skim milk. I couldn't stand it.

In my third year of college, my younger brother Billy contracted leukemia and his condition slipped rapidly. I wanted to go home and be with him, so I arranged my schedule to graduate in three years and a summer.

It was a difficult experience for me because everyone seemed convinced that there was nothing that could be done to save Billy. They said, "It's terminal and that's that." But it's not in my nature to give up without a fight, so I tried like hell to find a doctor who could find a cure for his condition. Despite everything, he died five months after he was first diagnosed. Years later, I named one of my sons after Billy, and happily, he's quite a lot like my brother was—a good, sweet guy.

I managed to make it all the way through college without losing my virginity. When I told a buddy of mine about this, he took it upon himself to correct the situation by taking me to a brothel where he was a regular. He picked a lady for me, and it looked as if I was going to finally do the great act for the first time.

However, once I was alone with this woman, she completely upset my equilibrium by asking, "What kind of love do you want?"

I knew so little about sex, I couldn't even grasp the idea that there was an assortment of options to choose from. I answered in my suavest voice, "What do you recommend?"

"How about 'Around the World?'" she asked.

"I don't know what that is," I told her, "but if you recommend it, sure."

"Around the World" turned out to be this: you started kissing her at one place and then went all the way around her body until you got back to the starting point. Being a considerate kind of a guy, I thought at least I should be giving her some pleasure too. So I began touching her and exploring her. I was just beginning to feel I was getting the knack of this when she suddenly said, in a very cold voice, "Watch your nails, sonny!"

This so shattered my poise that I grabbed my clothes and ran, putting my pants on as I went. That was my one and only experience in such a place.

My first job after college was in a telephone boiler room where a group of high-pressure salesmen tried to sell questionable stock to widows. I was the guy who delivered the stock. Soon, though, I abandoned the boiler room because I heard about a program at Macy's called the Executive Training Group. This turned out to be quite a rip-off. They recruited college graduates, sold them a bill of goods about executive training, then stuck them on the sales floor for the Christmas rush. But I was making twenty-five dollars a week and, since it was the depression, I was delighted just to be working.

My next job was in the art department of an advertising agency where it seemed that my chief duty was to remove excess rubber cement from storyboards. I got to be an expert at rubbing that stuff off. At the same time, I was going to Columbia and Pratt Institute taking graduate art classes. I was beginning to admit to myself, though, that there was something lacking in my talent. I would be drawing in class and look over the shoulder of the fellow next to me. It always seemed his artistic ability flowed so naturally while everything for me was a struggle.

Fortunately, the boss at the ad agency took me under his wing. I was pulled out of the art department and allowed to dream up gags and gimmicks for radio shows. I seemed to have a knack for getting people's attention—which is what advertising is all about.

During this time, I learned some tricks I was to use later, from a strange character named Curt Odin. Curt was a freelance idea man who kept trying to sell me on various ad campaigns. I ignored him and wouldn't return his calls. One day, in the mail, I received a wastebasket. In the wastebasket was a letter, torn into a hundred pieces. I took an awfully long time to put it together and found it was from Curt Odin. It basically said, "You idiot. I guess this is the only way I can get your attention." Later, when I was trying to get sponsors for my radio shows, I used the wastebasket trick—and it worked.

One of my own early stunts involved trying to get Philip K. Wrigley, the chewing gum magnate, as a sponsor. Wrigley was a copywriter's dream because if you approached him in the right way, he would bring you to Chicago and hire you to do a lucrative advertising campaign. I tried the normal avenues of calling and writing, but he didn't respond. Finally, I got an old plank that looked like part of a park bench, and I stuck onto it a few pieces of chewed gum. I wrapped up the whole thing and mailed it to Wrigley with a letter that said, "I have had these analyzed, and NONE are Wrigley's. Let our radio show correct this situation." That gag did the trick and he called me. Alas, for some reason, he never sponsored our show.

My fondest memory of advertising was when I worked as a script boy for Eleanor Roosevelt. She was doing a radio series called "My Day." This must have been at the peak of her popularity, because FDR was running for his fourth term. One day when she came into the studio, there was a group of blind children who had come to visit her.

Apparently, it came to her intuitively that she should mingle with the kids. What she did was simply to walk among them, touching them all. As I watched her do this, I felt like I was seeing somebody who came straight out of heaven. The children responded to her touch as if it was a magic caress. She was no great beauty, and she had a high squeaky voice, but she exuded a gentility and nobility that I'll never forget.

Besides those few experiences, I didn't like the advertising business. I felt then, and I think it's even truer now, that advertising is often organized lying. You are pretending that your product is something it isn't. Or that it is more than it really is. The goal of the advertising man is to create clever deceptions. Consequently, I left advertising and opened my first office, Allen Funt Productions, on Vanderbilt Avenue, near Grand Central Station.

My plan was to create and sell syndicated programs to radio stations around the country. It was slow going in the beginning—so slow that I sometimes had to borrow subway fare from my secretary. But eventually I sold several shows that became successful.

One hit show I dreamed up was the "Funny Money Man." It was idiotically simple. The disk jockeys at radio stations would form a "Funny Money Club" that listeners would write in and join. From the list of names, DJs would select people and ask them to send funny things of no actual value. The disk jockey might say, "Send me a check for a million dollars but don't sign it. In return I'll send you fifty-eight cents." It was amazing, but that program became quite popular and spawned a syndicated comic strip by the same name.

I actually had to lie in order to sell the show. I knew no one would want it until some other station had signed up. So I'd tell stations if they subscribed they would become "the 140th station," or some such thing. Finally, one of the biggest stations in New York, WEAF, signed up. We got them on a lie, but they never found out because we quickly sold the show to many stations.

For the first time in years, things were beginning to click for my production company. But then the war started and I knew I was going to be drafted, so I turned my fledgling business over to my sister to manage while I was gone. What I didn't know was that I was about to take the first direct step closer to the world of secret recordings—a route that would eventually bring me to the top of the world of television with "Candid Camera."

The Real Me?

THE self-image that people have is generally two-dimensional, consisting of what they *feel* about themselves on the inside and what they *see* of themselves on the outside.

Even though, inwardly, I've always felt fairly self-confident, I've always hated the way I look. I pass a mirror and I shudder; I watch myself on a TV monitor and I wince.

You'd think after many, many years a person would get accustomed to being bald. But I haven't. When I look in a mirror, I'm always surprised that I'm bald.

I've always felt that I look like a squat Dutchman. My family used to have a set of croquet wickets in human form, with bowed legs that you'd hit the ball through. That's how I picture myself.

Tailors hate to tell you that your legs are bowed. But whenever they would report my measurements, they'd cryptically say "BL-2" or "BL-3," which, I later learned, designated how many fingers would fit between my bowed legs.

I've spent most of my adult life dieting. Like many people in that predicament, I've got three entire wardrobes, consisting of "fat" clothes, "thin" clothes, and "medium" clothes (which get the most use). Sometimes I'll put on a pair of "thin" pants, leave the house, then go back because I know it will spoil my whole day if I think that I've worn the wrong pants.

The renowned caricaturist Al Hirschfeld claims that I'm the only person to have ever complained about one of his drawings in the *New York Times*. I said he made me look like a monkey. "God did that," replied Mr. Hirschfeld. "I only did the drawing."

I have that drawing on a bathroom wall along with other memorabilia. Some days I glance at the picture and find myself agreeing with the artist. But once in a while, I look in the bathroom mirror and decide that I don't look too bad.

Into Hiding

The U.S. Army never knew it, but Uncle Sam was indirectly responsible for the creation of "Candid Camera." After I was drafted in 1941, I was assigned to the Signal Corps where I continued creating radio shows. It was there that I got my hands on a German wire recorder. Up to that point any sound recordings were usually made in a studio using bulky equipment. This wire recorder, though enormous by today's standards, was the smallest, most advanced portable recorder of that time. And this gave me an idea.

A friend of mine in the Signal Corps, David Verne, was crazy about a girl named Helen. He absolutely worshipped Helen and hoped to marry her. Somehow, I was able to convince David to play a trick on her. With me hiding in the bushes nearby, recording every word of their conversation, David would tell Helen that he had met someone new and that they were finished. That trick, crude as it was, became the first gag in the "Candid" style. And in classic boomerang fashion—it backfired on all of us.

That fateful moment is branded into my memory. Here comes Helen down the street toward us. I'm hiding in the bushes with the wire recorder, and David is standing nearby. David must have been very nervous about the joke because when she was still quite a distance away, he shouted at her, "Helen, we're finished!"

There was a terrible silence. And as she continued walking toward him, the tears began to pour down her face. This, of course, was the response we might have anticipated. But her next line could never have been penned by any screenwriter because, as it turned out, she was crying tears of joy.

"Thank God!" she told him. "I was married last week, and I didn't know how to tell you!"

Now David was silent as he slowly turned to where I was hiding in the bushes. Then he stooped down to pick up a rock suitable for throwing and chased me all over the base. I could never convince him it wasn't all my fault.

That incident left me with mixed emotions, to say the least. I was just as unnerved as I was overjoyed. In the very first test of my new idea, it worked—but brought with it a swift counter-punch.

I didn't know it at the time, but I had just learned one of the risks of doing "Candid" gags: when you stop a stranger on the street, you never know where that person has just been or what they've just done. You might be dealing with a man who has just murdered his wife. Or, it could be a woman who was just fired from her job. It could be an escaped convict with a gun in his pocket. (Actually, we once photographed a man who was on the FBI's "Ten Most Wanted" list and convinced him to sign a release so we could use the footage.)

Even though I disliked the army, it did give me more experience in creating and producing radio shows. This came about
by chance, like so many other things in my life. I signed up for
Volunteer Officer Training which turned out to be as much of a
scam as Macy's Executive Training Group. The idea was that
you would become an officer and get the best assignments.
This never happened. Instead, I was eventually sent to Camp
Gruber, in Muskogee, Oklahoma, where I convinced the army
to let me do several radio shows.

One show I created was called "Behind the Dog Tag: The
Show that Makes GI Wishes Come True." As the title implied,
soldiers would write in with crazy wishes, and we would make
them come true. For example, one soldier wanted to go swimming in beer. We found a rich family with a swimming pool,
convinced them to empty it, then got a local brewery to fill it
with beer. Another GI wished he could "sleep until 10 o'clock."
Since he never specified a.m. or p.m., we hoisted him and his
bed far above our studio audience and left him there until 10
p.m. And, of course, we always recorded the whole scene for
broadcast.

The army also enlisted my help in raising money for war
bonds, and I had a fund-raising idea that we used several times
with considerable success. We would find a soldier who hadn't
seen his mother for many years. Then we would pack a theater
and seat the mother on stage. With a roll of drums, the soldier
would appear at the back of the theater in a spotlight, and we
would announce to everyone that the only way to reunite
mother and son was by purchasing war bonds. Each war bond
sold would bring the son one step closer.

People had to pay one thousand dollars for these war
bonds—which was a lot back then—but sales were brisk. As
mother and son drew closer to each other, the tears started to

flow. With each step they took, the excitement built until the place was in hysterics. When they were just ten feet apart, crying men and women poured into the aisles and carried the soldier to his mother.

Another radio show I did, called "The Gripe Booth," taught me a lot about people's reactions to being recorded. The idea for the show was that soldiers could come into the studio and complain about anything in the army without fear of repercussions. Maybe they hated their barracks, or the mess hall food, or being away from their sweethearts. However, as soon as the red light came on they became tongue-tied. My solution was to disconnect the red light and record them secretly. The conversations I obtained under these conditions were invariably more candid—a word, and a quality, I would come to value.

As soon as I was discharged from the army and returned to New York, I tried to create a radio show using hidden microphones. I didn't have an exact format for the show yet, but I managed to convince the Mutual Broadcasting System to underwrite my efforts with a check for $900.

My intent at that time was far different from what later became "Candid Camera." I wanted to create a program that would simply record the beauty of everyday conversation. The notion of having a chance to record people talking when they didn't know anyone was listening—pure eavesdropping—was what fascinated me.

At that time, my office was in the same building as the Conover Modeling Agency. "Conover Girls," as they were called, were the most beautiful girls in the world. It was common to see two or three of them in the lunchroom of our building, heads close together, talking intimately to each other. Nobody in his right mind could see this without wondering what they were talking about, and I daydreamed about hiding a microphone nearby in the soda-straw container.

When I got the money from Mutual, I did just that. I taped hours of conversation between these Conover Girls. And much to my disappointment and surprise, it was the most uninteresting garbage you could imagine. They went on and on about makeup or dating, or just the trivia of everyday life. It was a blow to find that even coming from these gorgeous girls, the conversation was quite mundane. Obviously, I was lacking some ingredient to make the concept work. Purely by luck, I discovered what that missing element was.

From my office window, I could look into a dentist's office in the next building. There are three things that I always hated about dentists. First, they fill your mouth with equipment, then ask you questions you can't possibly answer. Second, they have no concern about keeping you waiting while they answer personal calls at great length. (I had a dentist who was an avid golfer. He would load my mouth up with equipment, tell me to keep my mouth wide open, then he'd get on the phone with a friend and talk his way through eighteen holes of golf.) The third thing I noticed was that when the nurse is in the room, the patient is critical and outspoken; when the dentist walks in, the patient becomes intimidated and deferential.

I thought maybe other people had similar feelings about dentists, and so I arranged to hide a microphone near a dentist's chair. However, while I was still concealing the microphone, a woman walked in. Mistaking me for the dentist, she sat down in the chair and told me that she was having trouble with her wisdom teeth.

On the spur of the moment, I decided to see what would happen if I became the dentist. I picked up one of the instruments lying there and told her to open wide. I began to poke around in the woman's mouth while the appropriate dental phrases fell naturally from my lips.

After concluding my exam, I adopted my best dentist's tone and informed her, "I've examined you thoroughly, and I've discovered you don't have any wisdom teeth."

"Don't have any wisdom teeth?" she asked, simmering with anger.

I held my ground. "That's right. You must be mistaken. They just aren't there."

Before the situation went any further, the real dentist appeared and took care of her ailing wisdom teeth. But the encounter left me electrified. I had discovered the missing element needed to make the "Candid" format work—the introduction of a provocateur. Someone was needed to take the ordinariness of an everyday situation and push it one step further, into a scene, and in some cases even a spectacle.

The dentist's office incident had taught me something else. It showed me how well I could fit, chameleonlike, into different roles. Other than my brief —but fiery—stint as an actor in summer camp, I had little dramatic training. But I was blessed with a nonprofessional Brooklyn accent and the kind of face and manner which allowed me to be a bank executive one day and a plumber the next. People trusted me. In fact, as the world would eventually discover, people trusted me too much.

Soon, I became the instigator of all the gags. At first this was because I didn't have the money to hire anyone else to do it. But I also realized I had a talent to improvise and salvage a situation. We might be frustrated because we weren't getting an interesting response; I'd improvise a whole different setup on the spot.

Once, in the midst of an unrelated sequence, I stopped a man on the street and asked him what he did. When he said he was a bricklayer, I asked if he would seal someone inside a wall in my house. He agreed, as long as he could "leave an air hole."

Contriving situations by using a provocateur changed everything. Now I knew I could go out onto the streets of Manhattan, armed with a tape recorder, and be reasonably sure of getting something entertaining.

There was still one hurdle to clear, however. Everyone I spoke with at the radio networks said I would never get this idea past the legal department, unless, of course, the people we recorded had signed releases. But how, I argued, how can we catch them in a completely natural state if we first ask them to sign a release? The answer to this problem was, of course, ridiculously simple: record them first, *then* get them to sign the release.

Eventually, I completed several secretly recorded conversations and edited them into a sample tape. Mutual wasn't impressed, but the American Broadcasting Company bought "Candid Microphone" and scheduled it for broadcast in the summer of 1947.

I should say at this point that I can't even remember how the name "Candid Microphone" was chosen. It is, after all, a slight misuse of the word "candid." "Hidden Microphone" would have been a more appropriate title for the show. However, my advertising days had taught me that certain words grabbed people's attention, and the word "candid" was one of them. It was fortunate that "Candid Microphone" was what we chose because when we converted it to "Candid Camera," it worked even better.

As we frantically edited miles of tape for the first show, another important event was developing in my personal life. A year and half earlier I had married and now, my wife, Evelyn, was pregnant. We had been introduced by a mutual friend, and I immediately fell for Evelyn's beauty as well as her gentle reserve. I admired her determination and level-headedness. We were soon married and set up our home in a small apartment at Forty-eighth and First Avenue in Manhattan.

Late one night in September, 1947, Evelyn began to feel the first mild contractions of labor and knocked politely on the door to our smoke-filled living room where three of us were busy editing. "I really think we ought to go," she said.

"Just a few more minutes!" I snapped, hastily trying to finish one more piece. Soon, our departure couldn't be postponed any longer, and we grabbed a cab and sped across town to the hospital. The next day, as "Candid Microphone" aired for the first time, my first son, Peter, was born. It was a fitting entrance for Peter since he went on to work closely with me on many "Candid Camera" projects.

Immediately, our new radio show captured the public's attention, partly because it was so different from anything else on at the time. But it wasn't a blockbuster. Instead, it became more of an artistic triumph with a cult following. And some critics even saw it as the beginning of a new era.

After several months on the air, the *New York Herald Tribune* wrote that "Candid Microphone" was a show in which "everyone may tune in on their neighbors or, at any rate, somebody's neighbors and listen to their unrehearsed, unwitting, unsponsored remarks. It's a wonderful sport, like looking through keyholes but capable of infinitely greater variety." The same writer concluded with an accurate look into the future, "The possibilities are limitless: the prospect is horrifying. Wait till they get the Candid Television Camera. You won't be safe in your own bathtub."

Time magazine recognized the same possibilities and wrote, "With this new Machiavellian inspiration, radio crosses the last threshold of privacy. The whole country seems likely to be plagued with hidden microphones."

"Candid Microphone," unlike "Candid Camera" to follow, had an artfulness which bordered on theater. Since it was on radio, there was no opportunity to zoom in on a person's face and capture his expression. Instead, it all took place in conversation and the lack of conversation (sometimes the amazed pauses were funnier than anything else). I discovered that the tip-of-the-iceberg quality of the dialogue engaged the listeners' imaginations. What they couldn't see, they willingly imagined.

For example, we did a piece in which I put one end of a heavy chain around my secretary's ankle and the other end around the leg of her desk. Then I brought in a locksmith and told him I lost the key and needed the lock opened, "because it was her lunch break." There was a pause as the locksmith stared at the shackled woman, trying to hide his surprise. Finally he said, "I never saw anyone being chained like this before. Out West maybe..."

I soon learned that people were remarkably hard to rattle, particularly when you talked to them about their work. In one gag I went to a tailor and told him he had been highly recommended to me for a special job.

"I'd like you to make a suit for a kangaroo," I said. "A zoot suit with peg trousers."

There was a pause, and the tailor said, "A kangaroo. For heaven's sake. I've never tried anything like that."

"How many fittings would you need?" I continued.

"For a kangaroo? He's inclined to be a little wild, isn't he?"

"No. No. He's trained to box. But he only boxes other kangaroos."

There was another pause while he considered the matter seriously, then answered, "Roughly, for a kangaroo, I'd need three fittings."

"Give me an idea about the cost," I pressed.

"Gee whiz, I'm going out of the human line now, human beings, ah...I'd like to take it for just the experience and give you the cost later. I'll guarantee I won't rook you."

In other situations, "Candid Microphone" painted a portrait of New York in that era. There is one piece that was so beautiful I still remember every word of it, and it's been almost fifty years. I was walking down Sixth Avenue in Manhattan, and I saw on the second story a sign for an Italian violin maker named Giovanni Langeru.

I took my recording case and went up the stairs, introduced myself, and began to draw him out about his violin making. He wanted to tell me everything about the construction and the beautiful finish of his violins. He was bursting with pride as he exclaimed in his heavy accent, "Italian tone! Italian wood! Italian maker! But I'm an American, of course. I've been here for six years."

"It's true, you make beautiful violins," I said. "But I play the violin in vaudeville. For vaudeville I have to have a violin that is a little more showy."

"What do you mean, showy?" he asked uncomfortably.

"Could you make me a violin that has stripes, and maybe put some rhinestones on it?"

I thought this little old Italian would die. He handed me a violin and asked me to play. As I scratched out a few notes, he grabbed the instrument out of my hands and said, "Mister, if you play until the age of Methuselah, nothing will come out but lemon juice—without sugar."

In those early days, we became good at making people blow their tops. We went through all kinds of tortured rationalizations trying to justify what we were doing, but the fact is we pushed people too far.

One way to irritate people was to exaggerate something that was already recognized as a common annoyance. For example, in barbershops in those days, the barber would get you in the chair, then try to sell you a lot more than you wanted. So we decided to do a gag in which I was the barber, trying to sell customers everything imaginable.

Along came a little bald guy who sat down in my chair and asked me to trim the horseshoe fringe of hair around his head.

"How about a shave?" I asked.

"Just a trim."

"Maybe a manicure?"

"Just a trim."

I continued to try to sell him everything from massages to facials to shoeshines. And the response was always, "Just a trim."

Finally, I looked down into his shining pate and asked, "How about a nice shampoo?"

That did it. He didn't say a word. He didn't change his expression. He calmly took off the sheet, walked over to the counter where the tools were kept, and picked up a straight razor. He chased me around the barbershop, swinging that razor like he would cut me to ribbons! There were six or seven people on my staff hiding in the back, but no one came between me and the razor.

As our audience grew, we became aware that a significant group of listeners felt that the show was cruel—an opinion that persists to this day. I've always been very sensitive to that charge. But I've heard people say, and I've observed it for myself, that humor *is* essentially cruel. Unless the audience feels a certain superiority to what they're seeing, there is nothing to laugh at. So for a while, I allowed myself to be swayed by that credo.

As we grappled with the issue of cruelty during the early days, I got to know a performer named Henry Morgan. At the time, he was one of the top comics in America. But he had a very abrasive style; he was a knocker, he tore everything apart.

One day Henry said to me, "Allen, if you follow my route and show people in an unfavorable light, you'll have a short career."

Henry's advice persuaded me to evolve a standard for the material we used on the program. We decided to emphasize the heroic side of human nature. In the early days, we had a medallion we would give to people who agreed to let us use recordings of them on the show. On the back it said, "You were caught in the act of being yourself and were big enough to enjoy it." That, together with a careful emphasis of showing heroic and universal behavior, demonstrated to audiences that we really liked people.

Another reaction to our work that surfaced occasionally was the allegation that the skits weren't authentic, that they had been set up. This charge came from a sponsor named Mr. Woods who advertised his candy on "Candid Microphone." After the show had been on for several weeks, he came to me and said, "I just love the show, but you have to tell me the truth; is it on the level?"

I said, "Mr. Woods, you're killing me. Of course it is."

"I'm sorry, but I just can't buy that," he said.

That night I went home and brooded about this, wondering how I could prove it to him. The next day I placed a few calls and found that Mr. Woods was an avid golfer and that he often played at a certain course in New Jersey. I went to the course and planted a microphone on a tree on the pathway from the eighteenth green to the clubhouse. I convinced the golf pro to speak with the players as they came off the course. The pro was to say, "I saw you start out, and you were going great. What happened?"

The excuses clearly showed that golfers possess active imaginations and great verbal skills. And among those we recorded was our Mr. Woods. When it came his turn to explain "what happened," he outdid himself. "The caddie wouldn't shut up." And, "The rough was too long." And, "The foursome before us didn't rake the sand trap." Everything was to blame except his own golfing ability. Once we told him about the "Candid Microphone," he never again doubted the honesty of our show.

In those days, the late forties, the public was fascinated by the idea of recording equipment that was so small it could be hidden. Remember, this was at the beginning of the Cold War and fears of the Russians spying on the U.S. were constantly on people's minds. Publicity for "Candid Microphone" always mentioned how the microphone was hidden. I would occasionally get contacted by agents from foreign countries who wanted tips on improving their surveillance operations. Strangely enough, the U.S. government never contacted me, at least not directly. However, I did one piece which brought me in contact with the Secret Service.

We hid our recording equipment in a car and drove to the White House to see if we could get in to talk to the president. We pulled up to the East Gate, where a guard stopped us. I said, "Is the president in? I want to see him."

"Just a second," he said, looking in the car window. "Who are you, sir?"

"I'm a taxpayer. I haven't got much time. Is the president in his office?"

The guard tilted back his hat and leaned his elbow on the car window. "I don't know where the president is, and you just can't zoom in. Have you got an appointment?"

"No, but he'll see me," I insisted. "It's half business and half pleasure. Just tell the president I'm here."

After a few minutes of discussion, the guard started trying to get rid of me without offending me. "Why don't you try the

West Gate?" he said. "Just drive up there, and tell them what you want."

"You mean you want me to drive around to the other side and just zoom in?"

"No, don't zoom in. You'll get shot."

We were pleased with that piece, but before we could use it on the air, we had to get government clearance. This gave me an idea for a second, related gag. Two days later, as I was shown in to see John J. Maloney, then head of the Secret Service, I switched on my hidden tape recorder. Also present in Mr. Maloney's large office were sixteen other officials and assistants, all of whom listened to the tape without cracking a smile.

When the tape was finished, Mr. Maloney rose from behind his desk. "No!" he said. "If we let you use a recording like that, in two days every crackpot in the country would be at the White House kidding our guards." He turned to one of his men and barked, "Tell the boys at the gates that if anybody else barges in to see the president, have them arrested."

The chief turned to me, a little surprised I was still in his office. Trying to end the meeting with a laugh, I said, "Listen, if you're not going to let me use that piece at the gate, can I use the recording I just made of me trying to get clearance from you? Would you like to hear that tape?"

"We don't need to," he said. "We made one of our own."

It turned out that they had bugged the room. Naturally, we compared notes about recording techniques. I must say, I was shocked to see how archaic their equipment was.

Many people in the surveillance field seemed bent on the idea of getting the smallest possible microphone and hiding it in a very unimaginative place. Early on I found that we could use the size of the microphone to our advantage. We often got the biggest microphone we could find instead of the smallest.

When it was very big, it was less recognizable as a microphone. We built several props that held microphones—telephones, ashtrays, lamps. Once we were doing a piece in a pawnshop, and we simply put the microphone on the counter in plain view and hung a "For Sale" sign on it.

"Candid Microphone" was a hell of a lot of fun, and it might have gone on forever if television hadn't come along. But, once again, luck intervened. I was contacted one day by a newsreel film crew. They wanted to film us as we did a "Candid Microphone" piece. I was mystified. "How're you going to hide the camera?" I asked.

"Don't worry," they said. "We'll get it out of sight."

They certainly did get the camera out of sight, and the little piece of film they made began a whole new chapter in my life.

What's in a Name?

MY BIRTH certificate reads Abraham Funt. My high school diploma reads Albert Funt. My college diploma is the most accurate; it reads Allen Albert Funt—which is the name my parents finally settled on.

My childhood friends called me Allie. But when my mother registered me for school, she pronounced it so it sounded more like Ollie than Allie. So throughout grade school, I was known as Ollie.

My sister called me Sonny. After a while my parents picked that up—so to the family, I was Sonny.

In all other cases, my name is simply Allen. Unless, of course, I'm doing a "Candid" sequence; then my name is Lester.

When I opened my first office on Vanderbilt Avenue, I needed a name on the door—but certainly not my name. We called a sign painter, and when he arrived, I recorded our conversation for "Candid Microphone."

"What name should I paint?" he asked.

"How about your name."

This really threw him off. "Why should I put my name on your door?" he demanded.

"It's only a dummy corporation," I said.

He didn't like that explanation. But after a call to his boss, he agreed to paint his name, Lester Kannon, on my door.

We left the name Kannon on the door, since it seemed as good as any. Months passed. Then *Life* magazine decided to do a spread on "Candid Microphone." When I told the writer the

Lester Kannon story, he suggested we get the painter back to the office the next day to pose with his brushes at our door.

That night I got a call from the manager of 52 Vanderbilt Avenue. He said someone had sneaked into the building and was painting our door! By the time I arrived, the name on the door had been changed from Kannon to Cannon.

It seems that when Mr. Cannon appeared on "Candid Microphone," he fooled us: he painted his name on my door, but spelled it with a K instead of a C. But when he learned he was going to be in *Life*, he wanted it spelled correctly.

For forty-five years, I've used that guy's name in my stunts. And I always spell it with a C.

"Candid Camera" Is Born

CHAPTER THREE

In the summer of 1948, I screened the newsreel footage of "Candid Microphone" for ABC and got the green light to begin producing a television version of my hit radio show. The catch was, they wanted the first episode delivered to them in eight days! Adding even more pressure, the network informed me that "Candid Camera" would be the very first show broadcast by ABC when it went on the air on August 10, 1948.

As I madly began filming hidden-camera scenes, I discovered that "Candid Camera" would be fundamentally different than its radio counterpart. Now, of course, audiences would be able to see people's faces instead of just hearing their voices. It was the faces of ordinary people—confronted by extraordinary events—that would captivate viewers for years. These faces were filled with surprise, with bewilderment, with thought— and, at times, with anger.

"Candid Camera" quickly showed me the enormous power of televised images. For example, the most popular piece we ever made boiled down to three seconds of film in which not a word was spoken. All we show is a human face displaying an array of emotions.

Of course I'm referring to "The Talking Mailbox." In that gag we planted a speaker in a small mailbox attached to a light pole in Manhattan. As people posted letters, we tried to draw them into a conversation by saying things like, "Have you seen the mail truck? I haven't been emptied yet." One man who approached the mailbox was a crusty New Yorker. Everything about his manner showed that he was someone you shouldn't fool with. Yet, when the mailbox hailed him and asked him to open the lid and speak, he obeyed.

In the climax of the scene, our subject noticed a passerby giving him the eye. Trying to prove his sanity, he said to the mailbox, "Here's another guy that don't believe there's someone in the box." And from then on, the box didn't say another word, even though the man pleaded, "Speak up!" The look on this man's face struck a deep chord with the public. And, today, decades after that piece was first broadcast, wherever I go in the world, people tell me how much they loved the talking mailbox.

We had been producing "Candid Microphone" (which continued to run along with "Candid Camera" for another year) from the one-room office at 52 Vanderbilt Avenue that we shared with an accountant. Now that our budget had gone from $900 a week for the radio show, to $5,000 a week for the TV program, we moved into a duplex office overlooking Central Park. We also increased the staff. A few of the more colorful people were Phil Pollard, a writer and idea man; Sonny Fox, a production assistant I hired because his mother knew my mother (he went on to become a successful host and producer of kids' programs); Al Slep, a publicist; and Nina Heberer, our secretary. We were a tight-knit group of oddballs who worked long hours, driving other tenants crazy with the stunts we pulled.

As we began filming pieces for "Candid Camera," we discovered that hiding the camera wasn't the hardest part of our job. All we had to do was put the camera behind a folding screen and shoot through a two-way mirror set into one of the panels. People just weren't curious enough to nose around. (Children, on the other hand, were much more perceptive and weren't afraid to ask questions if they saw something unusual.)

Lighting the scenes was much tougher. Since the film speed in those days was slow, it required a lot of light, which drew curiosity and suspicion. To deal with this problem, I created a distraction. If we were filming at a lunch counter, I'd conspicuously light another corner of the restaurant, along with the area where we planned to be filming. If the other area was even brighter than ours, then our lights seemed much less suspicious. If someone did ask about the lights, I'd just say in a tone of authority, "They're fumigating the place." Or, "The painters are here." The important thing was to have a quick answer and deliver it confidently.

With the camera in place, and the area lit, we waited for the right person to come along. The waiting was the most excruciating part. I remember one stunt in particular involving a plumber. We were going to tell him we were having trouble with the water—the hot faucet gave cold water, and the cold faucet gave hot water. Imagine seven of us sitting in a room doing nothing except waiting for a damn plumber to arrive. At any moment he might walk in, and we'd all have to spring into action. But the whole day might pass without one of the plumbers we called showing up. It was enough to drive us mad.

Sometimes out of impatience, we would abandon the gag and make up something completely different. Eventually, I learned to trust the law of averages. I knew that almost every day, if you waited long enough, you'd get one useful piece. And often, it would come along just when we were ready to quit.

While we waited, I was constantly on the lookout for potential subjects. If you asked me to describe the perfect person for "Candid Camera," I'd say he's fortyish, a little overweight, and balding. When I saw one of those guys come along, I'd snap to attention.

But I couldn't be scientific when selecting subjects for the show. I had to let my hunches guide me. I've been a big hunch player all my life—and they rarely let me down.

After I spotted a potential subject, I'd engage him in a little warm-up talk. Sometimes I'd just ask him for the time of day. There are some people who seem annoyed by such a simple request; others who politely tell you the time; and a few who will offer a lecture on the benefits of wearing a watch. I'll take the grouches and the lecturers—the middle group is of little value on "Candid Camera."

Once I lined up a good subject, I'd give the signal to start the cameras rolling.

Choosing the right signal for the cameraman turned out to be another challenge. No matter what we tried, the cameraman forgot the signal, or I forgot the signal, or I forgot to give the signal. We even rigged up a button for me to press. Of course, then I'd forget to press it.

The best signal I stumbled upon, and used for twenty-five years, was to clear my throat. It was simple and didn't create any suspicion. Recently, I was at dinner with some "Candid Camera" people when I happened to clear my throat. Everyone jumped.

Assume then that the subject looked right, I'd given the signal, and the cameras were rolling. It was then up to me to make the piece funny and entertaining. How did I do this? I used what some say is my strongest talent—improvisation.

Our style of improvisation is both frightening and exciting. You're interacting with a person you know nothing about in a tension-filled state—like being in a play for which there's no script. And, on top of everything else, you must push that person right to the brink.

I wasn't the only provocateur we used. Later, when "Candid Camera" was a big hit, we hired some top actors to work with us, but many of them were really not good for our purposes. That's because they were used to playing scripted roles.

On the other hand, I'm not an actor, so I could be myself in our "Candid" scenes. And people believed me in many different roles. I've often said that if you met me and ninety-nine other people at a party, I'm the one guy you would never remember.

Improvising was one of the great joys of doing "Candid Camera." Later, when I watched myself on film, I was surprised at the things that came out of my mouth.

One such line was spoken to a man who approached me as I played the part of a clerk in a lost-and-found department. He had telephoned to see if we had found a pair of shoes he left on a New York commuter train. On the phone I told him that, yes, the shoes had been found. But when he arrived at our office, I said we had lost the shoes.

This gentleman seemed simultaneously amused by the absurdity of the lost-and-found department losing something and angered by the loss of his shoes. Finally he said, with more than a touch of sarcasm, "Well, if you happen to trip over them, please let me know."

I answered, "Sir, that's one thing about our department. Once we lose something, it stays lost."

It wasn't a great Hollywood put-down. But life's moments are not scripted by Hollywood. And besides, it kicked the scene into high gear as he showed a new range of emotions—all of which we recorded.

Dick Christman, who was an early addition to our staff, was also good at improvising. When I met him, he was a travel agent, and I was trying to buy an airline ticket. He recognized me and began to give me a slick double-talk routine about all the choices I had. What class seat did I want? What did I want for dinner? How much leg room would I require? What did I want to read on the plane? When he got down to asking me what kind of an engine I wanted the plane to have, I realized what he was doing.

"Your audition's over," I said. "You're hired."

Dick had no acting background, but he was perfect for "Candid Camera." He had a silly, childish sense of humor. In fact, he was a bit crazy. One of the best sequences he did was almost totally ad-libbed. We set up our cameras in a shop that sold all kinds of coffee. I was behind the counter, waiting on a customer, when Dick came barging through the door.

"Can I help you?" I asked him.

"I've warned you before," he shouted. "You're not getting away with it this time. I'm checking all your coffee."

He rummaged around in the coffee, pulled out a handful of beans, and ate one. Then, without a word, he fainted dead away. In the film you can see the customer stiffen as he watches this guy fall to the floor at his feet.

A few seconds later, Dick got up rubbing his face and said, "That's strong coffee!" Then he turned to the customer and tried to get his opinion, by asking him to eat a few beans. All the guy could say was, "I had some this morning, and it was fine."

Dick was always eager to get ahead and a natural practical joker. A few years later, we pulled a good one on him.

In those days, television shows had a single sponsor, and ours was the Philip Morris Company. It was our habit, as we traveled around the country, to pay our respects to the local distributors and managers of Philip Morris to make them feel important and thank them for their support.

We had just finished a week of filming in Detroit, and I was coming down in the hotel elevator with a couple of staff people. The door opened, and a woman stepped in who fit every Hollywood image of a hooker. There was absolutely nothing else she could have been.

She recognized me and said, "Allen, you can't know how much joy you've brought into my life. Isn't there *some* way I can repay you?"

We laughed a little bit, but as we continued down on the elevator, I told her I had an idea. I said to my buddies, "Go find Dick and tell him we ran into the wife of the sales manager of the Philip Morris Company, and we're going to have a meeting in my room in about ten minutes."

Dick arrived first, then the prostitute came in. She sat down, and Dick found a way to sit next to her and make small talk. After a few minutes, she looked around and said, "Fellas, in my business, time is money. When do we start screwing?" Poor Dick couldn't believe it. He was sure we were recording him.

Another aspect of "Candid Camera" we were still perfecting in those early days was the "reveal." This was the moment we told the subjects it was all a joke and they were going to be on television. (In later years the reveal was done with the trademark phrase, "Smile! You're on 'Candid Camera.'") This required delicate handling, but if done right, it was the best moment of the scene.

The reveal was hard to capture on film because the zoom lens had not been perfected yet. To go quickly from a wide shot to a close-up, the cameraman had to actually remove the wide-angle lens and attach a telephoto. This wasted valuable seconds.

I dreamed up a turret-style attachment for our cameras which held three lenses—wide, medium, and close—and hired an expert in the field to build it for us. The turret could be turned by the assistant cameraman just as the subject was told he was on "Candid Camera." We got so good at using the turret that we only lost six frames between the wide and close-up shots.

Occasionally, the reveal brought no reaction at all; sometimes people went into a rage. Often they tried to run away (so I learned to latch onto them and keep them in front of the camera). But most of the time, they collapsed into fits of laughter, hiding their faces and pounding the table and even hugging me.

After the reveal, we still had to get the subjects to sign a release which gave us the right to broadcast the film. In most cases, this was surprisingly easy. We gave each of them a check for $50 and the "Candid Camera" medallion. People kept those medallions for years. In fact, they often kept the checks too. Over the years, our books were thrown $50,000 out of whack by people who didn't want to cash their release checks. Instead, they framed them as souvenirs.

I'd be lying if I said everyone was a good sport about being caught by our hidden cameras. One notable exception was also the most painstaking and expensive piece we ever shot. It took place at a racetrack. We decided we were going to make someone lucky for a whole day. We positioned a member of our staff next to one particular lady. He told her he knew all the horses, and he would pick a winner for her. Then we bought a ticket on every horse in the race, so we had a winner for her no matter what. We did this all day, through nine races. But, when we told her it had all been a gag, she refused to sign a release. Even when we assured her she could keep the winnings, she wouldn't change her mind.

In another case, a young woman balked at signing a release and said, "I'll take it home and think about it." Each time we called her, she said, "I haven't made up my mind yet." It got closer and closer to our air date, and she was still "making her mind up."

Finally, I told someone from our office to find out where she worked. It turned out she was a receptionist in a company that had seven attorneys. Apparently she made the release a company project, and the attorneys were advising her to hold out for a larger payment. I was so angry at being manipulated by a bunch of lawyers that I dropped the sequence entirely.

Such frustrations conspired to make "Candid Camera" an unusually difficult show to produce. We often filmed forty hours a week, because it took as many as thirty tries to get a single piece that was usable. Then the lengthy editing process began. In between everything else, we had to do the creative planning for the following week's show.

In those months after the first "Candid Camera" episode aired, I was also still producing "Candid Microphone." On top of that, I was trying to find time to spend with my wife and one-year-old son. You would think this schedule wouldn't allow me time for anything else. But there was still one important thing to do—worry. I worried continually what kind of reception my new show would receive.

I've always been a worrisome guy. I've never started new projects with that great confidence of someone who says, "I can do it!" Somewhere in my early years, my parents had failed to endow me with a strong feeling of self-worth. To be fair, they had tried to be supportive—but they weren't very convincing.

Back in the days when I still wanted to be an artist, my mother had a way of *trying* to tell me how good I was. One day she had a few of her friends visiting and she boasted, "Allen just won second prize in a poster contest."

I said, "Mom, I'm not going to let you say that unless you point out there were only three people in the contest."

Later, after "Candid Camera" became a hit, I used to call my mother and say, "What'd you think of the show?"

"Well, your name was nice and big," she'd say, referring to the opening credits. I should have known better than to ask. It's a cliché, but it was true of my Jewish parents—they wanted me to be a doctor or a lawyer or even an accountant. But a television producer? It was too hard for them to comprehend.

My mother wasn't the only one who lacked enthusiasm for my creation. My own friends were highly critical of the "Candid Camera" concept. They felt that hiding a camera or a microphone was sneaky and unethical. One of my dearest friends was David Susskind, who had a popular TV talk show in New York and produced movies and plays. He kept saying, "Allen, you have too much talent to do a show like that. I'll help you get into anything you want. But forget this idea, it's no good."

I resented this terribly. I felt like saying, "That's great advice coming from a guy who never had an original idea in his life." David mostly did adaptations and restaged the classics.

In my darker moments, though, I had to admit that part of me agreed with these detractors. I kept feeling that I should be doing something more important with my life. For these reasons, I always tried to inject meaning into the show and give it some artistic interest. I once tried an experiment that even David Susskind might have approved.

We hired one of the major playwrights of the day, William Saroyan, to create a drama that we could compare with the same scene in real life. I admired Saroyan because his works seemed so full of hope and optimism.

I asked him to write a scene set in a furniture store that sold on credit. When a man came in to make a payment, he was told that an anonymous benefactor had paid off his entire debt. Saroyan wrote several playlets on that subject, and each contained a kind of heroic theme. In one scene, the character refused to accept the credit and gave a rousing speech. "I don't need anyone else's money. And if that day arrives, I'll come begging with my hat in my hand." It was moving—but as it turned out, not very accurate.

We took our cameras to a furniture store and filmed how real people reacted to the same situation. I'm sad to report there were no heroic reactions of "I want to pay it myself!" Some of the people were a bit confused, but all of them accepted credit from the unknown benefactor and beat a hasty retreat out of the store.

That experiment taught me that even as talented a playwright as William Saroyan would find it difficult to predict the behavior of real people. And for my taste, the "Candid" scenes were vastly more entertaining than the scripted drama.

Saroyan wasn't the only playwright interested in "Candid Camera." Clifford Odets contacted me for tips on how to secretly record his family, in hopes of solving a problem that plagues many playwrights. He wanted to create more believable transitions between sections of dialogue.

After playing the tapes, he told me, "When I listen to the conversations of real people, they don't use transitions. They change the subject in a flash. And yet, it's still believable." He went on to use that style in his writing, and it was magic. When you heard an actor on the stage jump from one thought to another without the slightest concern for continuity, it created an electrifying sense of reality.

While I kept trying to make our show more artistic, the sponsors had only one comment: "Keep it funny." The headman from Philip Morris would call me and say, "Al, we want comedy. Comedy! Can't you understand what I mean by comedy?"

I'd say, "Yeah, but some comedy has another —"

"Comedy! Make it funny!"

Each week for these first "Candid Camera" broadcasts I took our reels of film down to ABC's studios for a run-through. We had a simple set with a chair for our host, Ken Roberts, and a picture of the skyline of New York in the background.

In those days, all the various elements of the show—clips, narration, sound effects—were synchronized on one master reel. The music was done live by a staff orchestra. They were wonderfully talented musicians, but they weren't highbrow at all. Indeed, they were the kind of guys who, if they had a few extra minutes, would read a racing sheet. During the run-throughs, I used these musicians as my test audience. If they didn't laugh, I'd tear out a piece and use something else.

Over the years I came to rely on several people I considered my most reliable critics. When I moved to Westchester County, and commuted into New York City, one of these critics was an attendant in a tollbooth. On Monday mornings after the show aired, that toll taker was the most important critic in America for me. It wasn't so much what he said, but what he didn't say that told me how he felt. If all he said was "Good show Allen," I knew it was a dog. But if he picked out something special and said, "I loved that piece! My wife and I died laughing," then I felt good all day.

Of all my early memories, none is more vivid than the day "Candid Camera" was ready for its first live broadcast. I felt honored that my show would raise the curtain on the ABC Television Network. What I didn't realize then was that this was the beginning of more than forty-five years of television for me. And, as that great moment in my life approached, what was I doing? Worrying. Worrying that the show wouldn't go smoothly, that people wouldn't think it was funny, that the sponsors wouldn't support it, and that the critics wouldn't like it.

Sitting on the set, with my head full of worries and my stomach tied in knots, I was about to discover something about myself for which I've always felt very fortunate. As the stage manager finished the countdown and signaled we were "on the air," all worry and nervousness left me. It was as if someone threw a switch. When we were on the air, I was "on"—completely in the moment.

In the weeks that followed, newspaper and magazine critics waged a lively debate about the worthiness of "Candid Camera." Many of them loved the new show. *Time* wrote, "Funt is a highly resourceful ad-libber, and his victims are life itself, about as pure as the screen can ever catch it." *Variety* said, "'Candid Camera' is even better as a sight-and-sound presentation than it was as an AM (radio) attraction." *Billboard* was even more enthusiastic: "It proved a highly entertaining stanza with a genuine flair for bringing out the human in human beings." The writer's summation: "'Candid Camera' deserves a long life."

I wish I could say that these reviews were the ones that stayed with me. Unfortunately, the words that lodged close to my heart, and angered me for a long time, came from the *New Yorker*. The *New Yorker* always felt it was slumming when it wrote about me or my show—or most things on television. Some years later the magazine did an in-depth profile of my career which presented me alternately as a genius and a menace to society.

The *New Yorker's* first comment on "Candid Camera" came from Philip Hamburger who wrote that the show was "sadistic, poisonous, anti-human, and sneaky." By the end of the review, however, he managed to contradict himself. He said that despite my attempts to embarrass people, I actually demonstrated that human beings are "fundamentally decent and trusting."

If nothing else, my objective in making "Candid Camera" was to show people as heroic and able to overcome the small crises in life with grace and ingenuity. Over and over again, we showed scenes of people striving valiantly against the obstacles we put in front of them, then being good sports when we revealed the joke.

The response from viewers was not mixed in the least. They loved "Candid Camera." And as long as they tuned in, we were employed. The show was shuffled around on all three networks, but it ran every week for nearly six years.

It was during this period in my life that I occasionally began to be recognized in public. This always seemed odd since the thought that I was becoming a celebrity baffled me. Celebrities, in my mind, were movie stars. I wasn't a movie star. I felt more like a gnome doing this show far away from the Hollywood pizzazz. But obviously I had misjudged the penetration of "Candid Camera."

Once, I was in a cab with the actor John Garfield on our way to a Yankees game. John was an extremely egotistical guy, and he apparently thought he should be recognized. But the driver saw me and he flipped. He went on and on about how much he loved "Candid Camera." Finally, John exploded, "What the hell's the matter with you? Don't you know who you have in your cab?"

In 1954, we left the network and began producing the show for regional syndication, which was actually quite lucrative. The slightly relaxed production schedule also gave me more time to spend with my family, which now included a daughter, Patricia, and a second son, John, in our house in Croton-on-Hudson. We had moved to the estate, called "White Gates" because of its enormous gated entrance, in 1951. During this less hectic period, I turned my full attention to fixing it up and creating some special projects for my growing family.

The house itself was so big we counted the fireplaces, not the rooms. (There were nine fireplaces.) The basement housed my workshop where I sculpted busts of all my children and built large marble-inlaid redwood tables. Upstairs, I created a playroom for the kids which was first a ship's cabin, then a space capsule, and finally a general store.

The project which grew to the most enormous proportions was our model train set. I began with the idea that every kid should have a model train to play with, and I turned out to be that kid. In the upper floor of one of the many buildings at White Gates, I began laying track and building bridges. Before I knew it, the huge room was covered with a train layout that included multi-leveled intersections, mountains, lakes, woods, and cities—and miles and miles of electrical wires which became hopelessly tangled. I'm told that my children avoided the place for fear they would get lured into tracing wires or assisting in something that would take all day. At times I disappeared into this building in the morning and emerged, exhausted, after midnight.

When my son Peter reached grade school, sports began to dominate our household. We already had a pool and a tennis court where I engaged in marathon matches with Peter or whomever was visiting. Later, I built a regulation-sized basketball court and spent many afternoons either playing in, or refereeing, five-on-five full-court games. When football became Peter's passion, we converted a riding rink into a full-sized field. Golf presented a special challenge. It was easy enough to designate a hillside as a driving range, but I couldn't think of an easy way to pick up the balls once we drove them. I dodged this problem by buying about five thousand used golf balls from a local range. We spent a happy summer driving them into a pasture where the horses stomped them into the ground.

Most of these special projects were accomplished with the assistance of a fellow named Rocky Caputo. He was a mason by trade and spent the week laboring on construction sites around the New York area. On weekends (later he joined us full time) he worked with me building structures, remodeling houses, or creating horse trails. As my property grew from the initial purchase of 10 acres, to 18 and then more than 100 acres, Rocky and I blazed miles of trails through the dense Hudson Valley woods. After clearing the trees and pulling the stumps, we dragged a grader behind a Jeep. We became increasingly reckless in this activity, often getting the Jeep so mired in mud that we had to connect its winch cable to the nearest tree to drag it out.

Rocky worked for me almost the entire twenty years we lived at White Gates. As we labored shoulder to shoulder building a three-story tree house or creating a hilltop pergola (from which the view of the Hudson River was unsurpassed), I realized this remarkable man, who spoke in "dese, dems, and dose," could make or fix practically anything—including my spirits. In our years together, his loyalty became so strong that, if someone crossed me, he only half-jokingly would hint that he'd arrange to have their legs broken or that someone could drop a match in just the right place. While the offers impressed me, I never took him up on them.

One of our neighbors during this time was none other than "The Great One," Jackie Gleason. He lived about a mile and a half away in a house built of imported Swedish lumber and Florentine marble. He retreated there when he wasn't doing his show.

Gleason had heard that I lived nearby, and one day he dropped in for a visit. I was out riding when I looked up to see a huge purple Cadillac El Dorado, top down, cruising up the drive with the great man at the wheel. He was wearing a cowboy hat, and the famous Jackie Gleason grin was stretched from ear to ear. At his side sat a stunning blonde, whose name was Honey and who never stopped giggling the whole afternoon.

Gleason usually had his first drink early in the morning and, since this day was well advanced, his depth perception was somewhat impaired. I knew this because of a short, but sturdy, retaining wall that ran alongside our driveway. As Gleason roared through our gates, he underestimated the width of his car and scraped his Cadillac against the wall. A lesser man might have retreated after the initial brush but not Gleason. It was his will against the wall's, and so he kept right on riding the wall for 300 yards until he made it to the house. For years I was reminded of the event by a purple line which ran the length of the wall.

Besides that remarkable entrance, the only other thing that I recall about Gleason's visit was that he wanted to play a game with my kids. He attempted to hypnotize my three-year-old son, John. He wasn't successful, but in his tottery state, with his big watery eyes gleaming devilishly, he nearly scared the day-lights out of John. We finally managed to separate the man from the boy, and we all watched, with a bit of relief, as Gleason and Honey and the huge purple car disappeared back down our driveway.

In the late fifties interest in "Candid Camera" began to pick up again because some of our pieces were featured on Jack Paar's show. Jack was a very big booster, and he even took part in some of the gags. This kept our concept in front of the public and led to regular "Candid Camera" segments on "The Garry Moore Show," a popular CBS variety show.

One day in 1959, my agent, Ted Ashley, called with news that another one of his clients, Bob Banner, wanted to coproduce "Candid Camera" as a half-hour series for CBS. The year before, Bob had helped get me on "The Garry Moore Show." He had a deal with several of Moore's regulars—including Carol Burnett and myself—that if we ever landed spin-off series of our own, Bob would get 80 percent of the profits.

Bob always struck me as a lofty professional with a church-like manner; his nickname in the industry was the Deacon. I hoped that his reputation for fairness might help me renegotiate our deal. Knowing that Ted Ashley would be of little help, since we were both his clients, I invited Bob to join me alone for lunch.

I sensed that the best approach was simply to plead my case without artifice or maneuvering. I told him, "Bob, maybe I just don't understand the business, but this eighty-twenty split doesn't seem fair to me."

He listened, stone-faced. When I was finished he simply said, "Okay. So what do you want?"

"Fifty-fifty," I said.

He extended his hand across the table, and we shook on the deal. That extra 30 percent probably added up to well over a million dollars. (Years later he got it back when I bought out his share, which by then had become worth many millions.)

I had tasted success before. I knew "Candid Camera" was a viable program with tremendous possibilities. But I wasn't prepared for what would happen when it premiered on CBS in 1960. It was an overnight smash hit. And it was the beginning of the most exhilarating eight years of my life.

Candid Persuaders

WHEN I look at "Candid Camera" kinescopes from the 1950s, I'm taken aback by some of the things we did, but none is more bothersome in light of today's sensibilities than hidden-camera cigarette commercials.

Our sponsor in the early days was Philip Morris. Because programs had but one sponsor, there was an incestuous link between the entertainment and commercial portions of virtually all shows. Even the most popular news broadcast of that era, "The Camel News Caravan" with John Cameron Swayze, featured cigarette logos throughout the program.

"Candid Camera" actually began each installment with a tight close-up of a lighted cigarette in an ashtray. After holding that shot for many seconds, the camera pulled back to reveal our host—actually a polite term for pitchman—Ken Roberts, puffing away. And when it was my turn to introduce the sequences, I'm embarrassed to say that I, too, was smoking fiendishly.

So tight was the sponsor's grip on our program that we were forced to edit the word "lucky" anytime it popped up in a "Candid" sequence. Philip Morris feared it would link us with the competition, Lucky Strike.

None of this would have made "Candid Camera" any worse than other programs of the day, except that we used our most powerful tool—hidden-camera photography—to sell tobacco products. Using the very techniques and style that made our show successful, I would engage unknowing smokers in a "test" of Philip Morris and other brands, winding up with our classic "reveal."

"We've got to make sure these tests are on the level," I'd tell the subject while sharing news that we were on television. That endorsement—the "Candid" verification of truth—made the commercials so effective then, and so offensive to me today.

Fortunately, our relationship with the tobacco industry ended after a few years. But before that, I was visited at my Manhattan office one day by the head of Philip Morris, who arrived in a magnificent blue Daimler convertible.

"Let me make this short and clear," he began, sitting at my desk while I sat in what was customarily the visitor's chair. "Last week I bought the General Cigar Company. All we need to bring cigar smoking back into vogue is to show that women really like cigar smoke; they find it masculine and think cigar smokers have great sex appeal. Get me some 'Candid Camera' commercials to prove this."

"I don't know if we can find such women."

"Listen, my wife hates my cigars, but my girl friend says she loves it when I light up. You bring me six good commercials, and the blue convertible is yours."

That was all I needed to hear. Within hours we were out blowing cigar smoke at unsuspecting women—and they all coughed, sneezed, and told me off in one way or another. Three weeks passed, and we were shooting a different piece in a supermarket when I noticed an attractive lady in the next aisle. I lit a cigar and gave it a try. To my amazement, she confided that her daddy always smoked cigars, and she loved them.

As we were getting a release, she made a confession. "My boyfriend is the head of the Philip Morris Company. I wanted to prove to him that I could do a good commercial, but I think if he sees this, he'll kill us both."

After that I got tired of looking for female cigar lovers.

Meanwhile, it's been thirty years since I gave up smoking, and I don't miss it a bit. But I still dream of driving on country roads in that blue convertible Daimler.

Entering the Golden Age

In 1960, CBS practically owned Sunday night. It had a lineup of some of the most popular shows in television's history, beginning with "The Ed Sullivan Show" at 8 p.m. and capped by "What's My Line?" at 10:30. But there was one weakness in this otherwise solid evening: the 10 o'clock time period had been dominated for years by NBC with the "Loretta Young Show." And it was into this slot, on October 2, 1960, that CBS put "Candid Camera."

This was a daring, strategic move. James Aubrey, head of programming for CBS, was gambling that TV audiences were ready for something different. He predicted that they would be drawn to a reality-based show about ordinary people.

Aubrey was right. Within weeks, the trades were reporting that "Candid Camera" was denting NBC's ratings at 10 o'clock. By December, 1960, our show was the fourth highest rated TV program in the country.

This was the middle of the Golden Age of Television—and I found the industry had grown up considerably since my entry into the business in 1948. Television now attracted the top writers, actors and producers in the country. Advertisers had discovered that television could sell their products in unprecedented numbers. And so they opened the tap, and money flowed into every area of TV production.

Despite the immediate acceptance of "Candid Camera," my first year on CBS was a stormy one. We were continually balancing our format, looking for the right mixture of "gab versus gags," as one columnist put it. Much of this balancing act was caused by a feud that developed between me and my cohost, Arthur Godfrey. I had sensed trouble as soon as I learned he was going to be on "Candid Camera." But the choice was not mine.

When we first received the go-ahead from CBS for a half-hour show, we began auditioning people to be my cohost. Among those we considered was a young comedian named Johnny Carson. I should preface this by saying that Johnny will vehemently deny this story. But the fact of the matter is, I interviewed him for the part and decided not to use him.

Johnny had just finished a popular quiz show, "Who Do You Trust," so his name was suggested as someone who could introduce the "Candid Camera" gags and keep the show flowing with easy banter. We arranged to meet. But I found that he didn't have a casual manner; he sounded too professional. We were looking for someone earthy and real, yet somebody who could talk about people in a loving and slightly philosophical way. Johnny Carson simply didn't suit our needs.

Of course, Johnny didn't suffer from this decision. He soon got "The Tonight Show," and the rest is history. In later years I was a guest on his show many times, but then Johnny and I had

Trying to strike it big in radio, circa 1946.

Editing "Candid Microphone" from miles of magnetic tape, at 52 Vanderbilt Avenue.

My parents, Paula and Isidore, with Evelyn and me at our engagement party in 1946.

Tight-knit oddballs: (from left) Al Slep, Phil Pollard, Nina Heberer, Sonny Fox.

Preparing for the debut of "Candid Microphone" in 1947.

On the traffic-free streets of Moscow in 1961.

Kids, in Russia, and around the world, speak a universal language.

"Candid Camera" medallion fascinates Russian youngsters. We posed as tourists, but how ▶uld we explain carrying 90,000 feet of film?

My chance to "coach" Yogi Berra and Mickey Mantle, on a golf course in 1962.

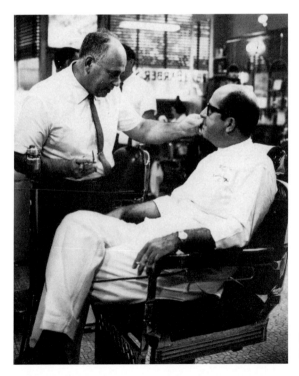

Comparing bald spots with guest Phil Silvers.

Mickey Rooney, with cowboy hat, does his "Candid Camera" spoof: "Just look at the moose and talk into the fishing pole."

The immortal Buster Keaton preparing for his lunch-counter gag: a brilliant series of spills and calamities.

With Jayne Mansfield in New Orleans, 1961. She told cabbies that her beloved poodle needed a ride to the airport.

Laraine Day, one of the first guest stars on "Candid Camera," in the early 1950s.

a parting of the ways. I had been invited onto his show and brought a "Candid Camera" clip to play. On the spur of the moment, he announced he was going to both introduce the segment and narrate it.

I had developed a very specific way of presenting "Candid Camera" pieces. By the time we went on the air, I knew every frame of every film clip. I also realized that people needed to be told when to laugh.

If the gag was that a guy was going to sit on a stool at a lunch counter and the stool would sink lower and lower, you'd have to say, "And you may notice something unusual about this stool. But this fellow doesn't notice anything until—" It had to be timed so that right after I say "until," he begins to sink.

So you can imagine how I felt when Johnny Carson wanted to narrate a film clip that he wasn't familiar with. I was actually bold enough to say, "Johnny, if you're going to narrate it, what the hell am I doing here?"

He said, "Allen, have you ever noticed whose show this is? You run your show, and I'll run mine."

And that was the last time I appeared on his show.

After ruling out Carson for "Candid Camera," we signed a contract with Eddie Albert for the cohost position. Eddie always struck me as being an earthy kind of a guy. But after we hired him, we shot a pilot that Bob Banner and I both hated. The folksy quality that was so apparent in person came across as being too stagy. When we broke Eddie's contract, he sued us for a lot of money—and won.

It was at this time that CBS came up with the idea of using Arthur Godfrey. They had the son-of-a-gun on a pay-or-play contract, and he was costing them $10,000 a week to do nothing. So here was an opportunity to get him off their payroll—and onto ours.

As soon as I heard that Godfrey was chosen, I died inside. I knew that having a cohost who was such a big name was asking for trouble. At the same time, we needed someone like Arthur Godfrey to attract an audience. He was very big in both radio and television, with two of the top ten TV shows of the 1950s. Anything Godfrey did seemed to be a hit. But to ask such a powerhouse to play second fiddle to me, on a show where he had nothing to do, was a nasty comedown.

To make matters worse, it was also an awful time in Godfrey's life. He had just had surgery for cancer, and every time he came to tape a show, it seemed he had just found out something about his condition. So the last thing he needed was for me to boss him around.

The press quickly got wind of the rift between Godfrey and me, and they played it up. The columnists would report that Arthur had said I was a tyrant and wanted to push him around. Then they'd call me and ask me to respond. It went back and forth like this for several months.

The main issue was that Godfrey wanted his part on the show enlarged. But at the same time, many critics were saying there was too much talk. The show, they said, stood or fell on the merits of the "Candid" gags.

As the feud grew nastier, there was speculation that one of us was going to have to leave. I was never very worried. I had nursed the show along for thirteen years, and there was no way they were going to get it away from me. I made this very clear in a statement to one reporter: "It would be harder to do the show without me than without Arthur." However, this prompted a brief rumor that I would be relegated to shooting the gags and leave the hosting to him.

As our first season moved along, things grew worse. Godfrey used to come in ten minutes before airtime as if he had just arrived from another planet. When it was time to introduce me, he did it with a little inside sarcasm. He didn't know what to call me—the coproducer or host or what. Finally he struck on the word "creator." But he had this way of saying it that made me sound like the guy who made the world in seven days. "Here is the *CREATOR*—Allen Funt!"

It was during this time that I became aware that Godfrey's dislike for me may have had roots in his anti-Semitic beliefs. He owned a hotel in Miami that didn't allow Jews. Furthermore, it was rumored that Lever Brothers, one of our sponsors, had anti-Semitic leanings. Bob Banner, with his businessman's sense of diplomacy, let it be known that Lever Brothers would side with Godfrey against me in any kind of a disagreement. Bristol-Myers, our other sponsor, was willing to back me. So for several weeks I had a very fine line to walk any time I was dealing with Godfrey, our sponsors, or CBS.

Ironically, the feud might have helped build our audience. In December, 1960, *Billboard* put it this way: "One of the major reasons that no one on the inside of 'Candid Camera' has bothered to deny the existence of a full-blown feud between Arthur Godfrey and Allen Funt is that you just don't shoot Santa Claus. Since reports of a tiff between the two gained wide circulation a couple of weeks ago, the ratings on the Sunday night CBS-TV rib-tickler have been higher than ever and production troubles have grown less with each succeeding week. Who could ask for a nicer Christmas present?"

I was in a state of disbelief about our popularity. "Candid Camera" had returned to network television as a ten-minute spot on Garry Moore's variety show, and many people predicted it wouldn't last thirteen weeks as a series. But there was another factor to account for our success, an important personality in this early mix. Her name was Dorothy Collins.

Dorothy had made a name for herself as a singer on "Your Hit Parade" with regular appearances on Garry Moore's show.

One night after Moore's taping, Bob Banner and I were talking about how we still needed a woman on the show.

Banner named a couple of comediennes who were popular at that time. But none of them struck me as just right.

"'Candid Camera' isn't geared that way," I said. "We need someone kind of apple pie-ish, fresh, next door-ish, like—like Dorothy Collins over there."

If hidden cameras had been capturing that moment, you would have seen us both do classic doubletakes. It was immediately clear that Dorothy Collins would be perfect.

When we asked Dorothy about joining our show, she paused and said, "I didn't know 'Candid Camera' was going musical." When we explained that we wanted her to become an actress in the gags, she quickly agreed.

On the premiere show, Dorothy appeared in one of our most popular pieces. We scouted for filling stations at the bottom of hills. Then we put Dorothy in a car from which the motor had been removed and let her glide down the hill and into the station. She instructed the attendant to check the oil. The looks on the attendants' faces when they lifted the hood and searched for the engine, were priceless.

Dorothy Collins went on to do several car-related gags, and it was soon evident that she was America's sweetheart. No one could ever be angry at Dorothy Collins. This was true even if she asked a man at a gas station to *change* the air in her car's tires. She explained that she was sure the air had become dirty, and very patiently, the attendant changed it. These car bits— the car with no motor, the split car, the sports car with the forty-gallon gas tank—were among the most successful stunts we did.

Elaborate jokes like this called for highly unusual props. Now that our show was a big success, the staff kept asking me, "Allen, why do you do everything the hard way? Spend the money, and go to expert prop makers. What do you care? The network's picking up the bill."

True, "Candid Camera" had hit the big time, and the money was there. But I had acquired an aversion to using successful people as suppliers. The top-dog guys didn't give me the enthusiasm I was looking for. I've always profited more by going to some little guy, for whom it might have been the biggest event in his life, certainly worth extra attention.

That's how we built the split car. Somebody told me about a bunch of hot-rod kids in Syracuse. They built a car that could split in two and both halves would then drive independently. We used it to fool a cop who was directing traffic—just split the car and drove it on either side of him. I'm not sure he ever recovered from the shock.

We once had a stunt involving trick suitcases, each with a uniquely crazy function. I wanted one to move on its own without anyone touching it. I wanted one to talk; one to leak water; one to open when you touched it. I went to a small prop maker, and when he found out they were for "Candid Camera," he put all his skill into it. I still have those suitcases, and they work just as well as they ever did.

In the winter of 1961, Arthur Godfrey taped a few dozen "Candid Camera" intros, then left to film an unrelated TV special in Africa. With Arthur on the other side of the world, peace returned to our set, and we were all able to concentrate on the show itself. The lack of gossip about the feud didn't hurt us at all—each week "Candid Camera" continued to appear somewhere in the Nielsen Top Ten.

The advantage of having a hit TV show is that the network and the sponsors leave you alone. This was during Bill Paley's reign as head of CBS. As long as "Candid Camera" remained a noncontroversial hit, I had little to do with Paley (although a year later, he would intercede on my behalf on a key programming decision). I dealt with Jim Aubrey, the head of programming. Aubrey was a colorful character, charming, but in a hardbitten sort of way like Clint Eastwood. His nickname was the Cobra—and he had the reputation of being fair but tough.

Aubrey and Paley nurtured "Candid Camera" to make it a winner. They patted me on the head and said, "Keep going. You're doing fine." Their only ongoing concern was that I would get too artistic. "Keep it funny," they'd say. "Keep it broad."

But as our ratings climbed, I kept searching for ways to occasionally step back from the broad humor that the network was advocating. One device we came to rely on for this purpose was music. With a musical accompaniment, we were able to interest audiences in behavioral studies, without the need for a formal gag or an instigator to keep the scene moving.

Perhaps the most memorable of these musical vignettes were four traffic cops, photographed in different cities, each with bold and distinctive traffic-directing gestures. In Reading, Pennsylvania, for example, one cop seemed to us to be a matador, challenging the cars and trucks as they bore down on his position in the intersection. We selected "The March of the Toreadors" to accompany his gyrations.

Among numerous other musical pieces were crying babies, mouths open and faces contorted, which we set to a heartwrenching operatic aria; dogs wagging their tails enthusiastically in time to an energetic march; and people walking down steps, punctuated only by a drum solo. These sequences showcased the fascinating variations in routine activities, with music providing a humorous twist.

During our run in the sixties, I was paid as the producer, performer, and 50 percent owner of "Candid Camera" with Bob Banner. While Bob had agreed to this split, it led to an interesting game of one-upsmanship. If I remodeled my office, Bob would remodel his—more extravagantly. If Bob got a new car—I'd get a better new car.

I wish I could say that success put me on top of the world. I wish I could say that having millions of people simultaneously watch my show did magical things to me. The fact is, I simply couldn't grasp the enormous power of television. Nor did I fully comprehend the penetration of the show. Some years later I got a glimpse of what had happened when I took a trip to a remote island in Hawaii. Shortly after I arrived, I was walking down a pristine beach when I heard rustling in the bushes behind me. As I turned, three little Hawaiian girls popped up and yelled, "Hello Allen!"

But in the early sixties, I had no idea what I was on to. Instead, I lived under a mountain of steady pressure. I felt like I lived in a tunnel that ran between our "Candid Camera" offices on West Fifty-fifth Street and the CBS studio.

As each season drew to a close, we began to run low on material we had stockpiled over the summer. This was a problem that would plague me every year. When it came time to make up the first show, we'd have maybe thirty pieces on the shelf. A professional would say, take a few of the best pieces and save them for later in the season. Not me. I was so concerned about getting the show off to the strongest start that I'd use all the best pieces in the first show. I assumed I would find a way to fill the holes later. I never could hold back.

This inability to plan ahead resulted in a weekly crisis. Every Thursday night, I'd look at the schedule and panic over what we would use for Friday's taping. Then I would spend one of a countless number of nights torturing myself, searching for a solution.

One Thursday night, we came up with the idea of doing a piece in an all-night diner, to be used the next day. "Lonesome"

George Gobel, the droll comic, played the part of a sleepwalker, and I was behind the counter as a cook. George wandered in, sound asleep, and sat down next to a truck driver. I kept telling the trucker not to worry. "He thinks he's at home in bed. So just don't scare him and you'll be fine." The truck driver played along for a few minutes, but when George started to lean on his shoulder, the trucker said, "If that guy tries to kiss me, I'll clobber him." It turned out to be one of the more popular pieces that year, and it certainly saved the week.

That experience didn't teach me a thing about planning ahead. If anything, our success in the diner made me even more confident about my hunches and last-minute "saves"— traits which would serve me well in the years ahead.

Censored! Censored!

"CANDID CAMERA" would seem to be a censor's nightmare. After all, our footage is raw, unscripted dialogue, straight from the pages of real life. And the people we confront—often blue-collar working folks—are put in tense situations. So you'd think there must be one deleted expletive after another.

In forty-five years of producing "Candid" programs, we've never had a serious problem with rough language. That's not to say we don't occasionally bleep this or that—but it's not an overwhelming concern.

In the earliest days of "Candid Microphone," our technique for dealing with profanity was to play the offensive material *backward*, which retained its length and tone but made it unintelligible. It was the audio equivalent of the #!()&*! used by cartoonists. This lasted until we learned that some listeners were taping our program and playing it in reverse just for the kick of hearing the obscenities.

I decided to record my wife, Evelyn, intoning in her most sultry voice, "Censored! Censored!" and we used that snippet of tape to cover the occasional four-letter word. It was so effective that we sometimes used the voice of the "censor" to spice up scenes in which nothing objectionable had been said.

By the time "Candid Camera" was born, we had polished our ethics and deleted only words that truly couldn't be broadcast. Of course, by then the network employed actual censors, who often struck me as overly protective of the airwaves.

Once I was talking about sports with kids at a kindergarten. One boy said soccer was the big craze, and he explained the rules—amusingly if not too clearly.

"Soccer is a dangerous game," he said.

"How so?"

"Well, if a guy tries to kick the ball and misses, he can kick you in the nuts."

The minute he said it, I had a vision of the censors convening in the boardroom at CBS, their brows furrowed as they debated the propriety of the word "nuts."

What else could a six-year-old say? He's not likely to know the term "testicles," and "balls" wouldn't have been much better than "nuts." But to bleep him would make it sound much worse than it really was.

The kid kept talking about soccer.

"There's one guy who doesn't have to worry about getting kicked in the nuts. He's the goalie. Goalies wear nut guards."

A few days later, I played the tape for a woman from CBS program practices. When we got to the word "nuts," she said peevishly, "Oh, come on, Allen."

"What's the matter?"

"You know we can't use that."

She went "upstairs" for a final decision, and in this case we won. CBS relaxed its moral vigilance enough to let that charming six-year-old say "nuts" on network TV.

And that's about as foul as the language on "Candid Camera" ever gets.

A Day With "Candid Camera"

I've been hiding cameras for so many years that it's almost second nature to me. But in the course of writing this book, I've tried to view my work from an outsider's perspective, and it seems, well, strange, to say the least. I find myself wondering if some readers are confused about how we plan sequences, select our subjects, and lure them in front of our cameras.

Recently I found a minute-by-minute description of the making of "Candid Camera" in a log I once had a crew member keep. It gives a portrait of a typical (if that word can be used about this line of work) day of filming with the "Candid Camera" crew back in the fifties.

Don't expect to die laughing at the gags. These are not highly memorable "Candid Camera" scenes. Instead you might be more amused at the bumbling way we often proceeded and how, at every turn, we were confounded by our subjects.

The scene is a Manhattan shoe store. The characters are Dick Christman, my right-hand man and crew chief; Arthur

75

Florman, cameraman; Howard Kuperman, assistant cameraman; Ralph Friedman, sound engineer; Tom Murray, idea
man and expediter; and Al Slep, production manager.

The log begins just after 9 a.m.

9:04 Dick calls Allen to check a suggested hiding place for
our cameras and mikes; it's one of the London Character Shoe
Stores. Allen says it sounds good, and Dick arranges to go down
to the store and look it over.

9:11 Dick, Art, and Ralph leave for the store. They check
photographic, sound, and program possibilities.

9:48 Dick calls Allen from the store to say it looks good
and tells Howard to bring the station wagon with the equipment.

9:55 The station wagon arrives at the location. The crew
pitches in to unload the camera, microphones, sound
recording equipment, and the concealment apparatus; plus
three crates containing miscellaneous items such as cables,
friction tape, extra light bulbs, raw film stock, and an assortment of tools.

10:01 One of the shoe salesmen says he's going to call his
wife and have her come down so she can be on television. Dick
explains that we never use people who know we're photographing them. The salesman looks hurt.

10:14 Arthur has had Howard set up the camera in a corner
at the rear of the store. A brightly lighted display nearby will
make our floodlights less noticeable. We'll have to lure subjects
into one of the three seats that are within camera range.

10:25 Ralph, his sound equipment hidden in a stock room,
is working on the concealment of the microphone. He tries
attaching it to a standing ashtray near the seats we'll be photographing, but it's too obvious. He runs next door to Whelans

drugstore and comes back with a box of Kleenex—a favorite hiding place for our mike. Dick says it won't work; a box of Kleenex on a counter or a table is one thing, but it would be too out of place perched on an ashtray.

10:41 Ralph comes up from the basement, carrying a display model of an ankle and foot, encased in a sock and fastened to a heavy base. He puts the display on a small table, lowers the mike into the hollow ankle and drapes an extra pair of socks over it. He asks Tom and Dick to sit in the seats and hold a conversation so he can check the voice level. He says it sounds all right.

10:56 Howard has placed the folding screen around our Mitchell camera and attached the two-way mirror to the opening in front of the screen.

11:09 Dick calls Allen to say everything is ready. Allen has a dentist appointment at 11:30. He tells the crew to start without him; he will join them after lunch. On the first try, Dick, posing as a shoe clerk, leads a man of about thirty-five over to one of the seats within camera range and suggests that the fellow take the "foot test." The customer is puzzled, but he agrees, and Dick puts him through a series of toe wiggles aimed at our camera. With Dick urging him on, the man bends his feet forward, backward, and sideways, and finally Dick tells him he's been performing the "foot test" for a television audience. The news takes a while to penetrate, but finally the man laughs loudly. Dick gets his signature on a release form. This first sequence is mainly to test the setup but may have possibilities.

11:22 Dick leads a young lady into camera range and finds that she wants to buy some slippers for her boyfriend. He clears his throat, the cue for the camera and recorder to start rolling, and suggests to her that she buy mismatched slippers—each one of a different size and color. The woman is cute, she's polite, but determined to get the slippers she came in for. Dick decides the sequence just isn't right...not enough fire. He leans over to the mike and says, "Cut."

11:40 The crew breaks for an early lunch because Allen is due at 12:30. We eat at a restaurant two doors away from the store.

12:20 P.M. As we start back toward the store, Ralph sees a cop making out a parking ticket for our station wagon. Ralph dashes over to him, but by the time he gets there, the cop has draped a ticket on the windshield wiper and sped away on his motorcycle.

12:40 Allen arrives, calls the crew out of hiding, and asks whether they've gotten anything. Dick describes the toe-wiggling scene. Allen frowns and shakes his head. "It doesn't sound right. It seems as if we make a guy look silly for no reason."

12:52 The crew has switched on our lights, and we're ready to shoot again. The store manager comes over and tells Allen that we missed a lot of wonderful characters during the lunch hour.

1:06 Allen leads a customer, a heavyset man, into camera range. Pretending to be a salesman, Allen picks up one of the store's foot-measuring devices. At that point, the customer shouts, "Oh, oh. Wait a minute. I've seen you on the television!" Before any of the crew can stop him, he turns to the rest of the customers in the store and shouts, "You know who this is? It's Allen Funk, from that whaddaya-call-it program...where he hides cameras." Allen takes the crew outside for a breather.

1:50 The last of the customers who'd been told about "Candid Camera" have gotten tired of waiting for the crew to reappear and have left. The store manager comes over and says that some of the customers we missed while we were gone were wonderful characters.

2:02 Al Slep phones from the office. He tells Allen that of the four sequences shot yesterday—for which everyone had high hopes—one is good, one is fair, and the other two are useless. Allen relays the news to the rest of the crew, and their spirits drop noticeably.

2:07 A man enters the store with his five-year-old redheaded son. The little guy is bright and talkative and looks like a good bet for a "Candid" portrait. Dick comes toward them, then steers the youngster into camera range. The redhead reveals quickly that he wants to be a puppeteer, "just like my daddy is," and goes on to say that he hopes soon to get an agent. Dick finds that the boy does imitations and persuades him to give his impressions of Milton Berle, Johnny Ray, and Jimmy Durante. At a suggestion from the father, seated just out of camera range, Dick tries to get the little fellow to talk about baseball. But nothing much comes of it. Dick asks him where he got his red hair. The boy says, "It came wit' the head." Dick seems to think this will make a fine closing line for the scene so, to make sure we have a good version of it, he asks the same question again and gets the same answer.

2:16 While the camera is being reloaded, the store's shoeshine artist, Willie, tells Allen that he wants to give him "the best shine in the world." Allen is skeptical, but Willie delivers as advertised.

2:31 A young man and his mother come into the store, and, without any guidance, take two of the seats within camera range. Dick pretends to be a salesman, and Allen takes a seat behind the two customers, acting as if he is waiting for service himself. The mother says she wants to return a pair of shoes the young man bought in the store yesterday; they have raised a blister on his foot. Dick starts to tell the mother he doesn't want to see the blister, but she wants the boy to show him. At that moment her son swings around in his chair and notices Allen and apparently recognizes him. He seems to be ready to blurt out the secret, so Allen gently but firmly puts his hand over the young man's mouth. Tom enters the scene, posing as a store executive, and orders Dick to look at the blister, under penalty of being fired. Allen stands up, takes off his coat, and drapes it over the boy's face to make certain the secret won't escape. The mother looks over at her son, suddenly notices the coat wrapped around his face, and is bewildered. Allen is about to tell her what's going on, when the son throws off the coat and says to Allen, "Let me tell her!" Then, "Hey, Ma! Ma! Don't you know who this is? It's that 'Candid Camera' guy." This looks like a good zany kind of scene.

2:46 The young man from the last episode asks if he can watch us catch some other people. We let him look on from a distance. Dick brings over an elderly man, seats him, and then calls Allen over. They are about to start a conversation when one of our lights burns out. This makes the customer aware of the other lights, and he asks what they're for. Allen says, "We're going to have the place painted." The customer nods, satisfied with the explanation. The light is replaced, and Dick and Allen pretend to be arguing about the type of shoe the customer should wear. He doesn't react, though, and they decide there's no point in trying further. Allen turns him over to a real salesman.

2:57 Allen spies a short man coming into the store, and Dick waits on the gentleman, who wants a pair of elevator shoes. Dick asks the man whether the added height the elevator shoes give him isn't frightening. "Don't you feel dizzy when you're that much further up in the air?" The man protests that it's only a matter of a half-inch difference, and he doesn't even notice it. Dick asks the man whether his wife likes the added height, whether he feels that he's towering over other short men when he wears the shoes, and so on. Allen says he doesn't think it will be a strong scene.

3:13   A pretty girl approaches Allen and asks, "If I buy a pair of shoes for my husband and he doesn't like them, will I be able to return them for credit?" Allen looks her over carefully and turns her over to a regular salesman. Tom says to Allen, "Why did you pass her up? She looked like a live one." Allen shakes his head. "She knew what we're doing. You get so you can tell the ones who are trying to fool us. They're always well groomed for the camera, and they come in with some ready-made idea like that business about the husband's shoes. One of the salesmen must have tipped her off."

3:27   A heavy rain begins and about forty people rush into the store from the street to keep from getting wet. The crew turns off the lights and prepares to sit out the storm. There's no chance to do any work with the store this crowded. The crew takes a break at the drugstore on the corner. When they return, the manager tells Allen that we missed some wonderful characters while we were out.

3:47   A man comes in, and Dick takes one of his shoes, asks him what kind of new shoes he wants, then goes off as if to fill the order. The plot is that we will photograph the man's indignation when Dick fails to return. Arthur shoots five minutes of the man waiting but no indignation yet. The camera is reloaded, which takes three minutes. To try to get a rise out of the customer, Dick walks past him idly. Still no reaction. Arthur shoots the full five minutes of the second roll, but the man doesn't change his expression. Finally Allen tells him what was going on and asks, "What were you going to do—just sit there forever?" "No," the man answers mildly. "I was going to wait another few minutes, and then I figured I'd just walk out."

4:10 A mother and her fourteen-year-old son come in to get the boy some blue suede shoes. Dick tries to persuade the mother that the boy shouldn't wear suede shoes. After considerable three-way discussion, Dick suggests that they all vote on the matter, and he tears a piece of paper into three parts, and each person marks an individual verdict on the secret ballot. Dick looks them over and announces that he, the mother, and the boy have all voted for the suede shoes. When Dick tells them they've been on television, the youngster looks very composed, but the woman lets out a laughing shriek and covers her face.

4:50 We're through shooting for the day. The crew is packing the equipment in the station wagon. Allen, Dick, Arthur, and Tom go back to the office to view the scenes shot the day before. When they arrive, the day editors are just leaving and the night editing staff hasn't yet arrived. Al Slep shows us yesterday's rushes. There's some discussion about each scene, but everyone finally winds up agreeing with Al's earlier evaluation of the material: one good, one fair, and two for the trash can. The night editors arrive, and Al turns over the two usable scenes to them to edit into final form.

5:37 Allen, Dick, Arthur, and Tom are discussing suggested hiding places for tomorrow. The secretaries and receptionist are leaving. The station wagon has returned, and the crew is bringing equipment up on the freight elevator. Back in the editing rooms, there is the blare of sound tracks being played over and over. Above the noise, Al's voice can be heard as he shouts at one of the editors, "No, I told you a hundred times! You can't have anybody using 'God' that way on television. Bloop it the hell out of there!"

The log ends there. But there is a note which states that the scene in which Dick persuaded the man to wiggle his toes was, as feared, too silly to be usable. The scene with the five-year-old impersonator was good, and we eventually used it. The mother and the young man who recognized me—the one whose head I threw my coat over—was a strong enough scene that we used it for the closing of our program. The exchange between Dick and the man who wanted elevator shoes was a tough call. We considered it for a while and finally discarded it on the basis that it was too unusual. The episode about the man waiting for ten minutes or more for his shoes turned out to be just as dull on film as it was in the store. We threw it out. And with it went the scene where Dick, the mother, and her son voted on the question of the blue suede shoes.

That was more than forty years ago. If we had kept logs of "Candid Camera" shoots in the years that followed, they, too, would be marked by great frustration, with constant starting and stopping. But over the years there have been several important changes in the way we work. Most notable, I believe, is that we long ago stopped shooting with so little structure. In that shoe store in the fifties, Dick Christman and I tried one premise after another based on the behavior of each customer. In later years we never worked without a specific "stunt" in mind.

As a network hit in the sixties, other things changed too. For example, locations were always scouted a day or two in advance, so crew members knew exactly where they were headed at 8 a.m. sharp. In 1966, we changed from black-and-white to color film. Shooting in color required brighter lights, which were harder to disguise.

In the early seventies we began using videotape in the field. Thanks to tape, we were able to do away with bright floodlights almost entirely. Tape also allows us to play back material on the spot. This is helpful in creative decisions, but it can be a curse in dealing with the public. Increasingly, we were asked by our subjects to let them see what had just been shot. But since most people don't like the way they look on TV, we had to adopt a white-lie policy of telling subjects that our "special tape" can only be played back in our studio.

The switch to tape also meant that a single cameraman could operate our photographic gear without the help of an assistant. Meanwhile, small wireless microphones became readily available. Some of these are so tiny and bear so little resemblance to larger mikes that they hardly need to be concealed at all.

One of our major achievements was to eliminate the two-way mirror (which blocked too much valuable light). We replaced it with our own invention—a slanted piece of clear glass onto which a graphic design is projected.

Here, revealed for the first time, is how it works:

Our camera, on a tripod, is hidden behind an ordinary folding screen. A rectangular hole is cut in the center of the screen, and into the hole is set a clear piece of window glass, angled at about forty-five degrees. Below the glass is a box containing a bright light. Above the light is a piece of translucent shelf paper, mounted on clear plastic.

The light shines up, through the shelf paper, and projects the pattern from the paper on the clear glass. Our unsuspecting subjects see only a screen with a strange colored pattern in the middle of it. But from the other side of the glass, the lens of the camera "sees" no reflection, just a clear view of the action.

One other thing caught my eye in reviewing the log from 1952: my own work habits. I was a bit startled to read about a "typical" day in which I arrived at the location at 12:40 p.m. True, I apparently had a dentist appointment that day, but I rarely missed time on one of our locations.

During the sixties, the pressure of our CBS schedule was so great that I often worked exclusively in our office editing footage and left the fieldwork to assistant producers. But with our feature films, cable programs, and all the network specials that followed, I made it a habit to be the first one at the location at 8 and among the last to leave after the final subject had been told to "smile."

Airline pilots describe their job as hours of boredom punctuated by seconds of stark terror. Making "Candid Camera" is similar: hours of waiting for just a few moments of excitement and hilarity. And, like airline pilots, we spend those hours of waiting in a state of constant readiness—readiness for what, we never know.

Pure Inspiration

I'M FREQUENTLY asked where the ideas for "Candid Camera" come from. In truth, I've thought up most of our stunts, although at times I've been helped by my talented associates, and by viewers offering suggestions through the mail.

Most of my best ideas for the show have come to me under deadline pressure—while driving to the office on the morning of a shoot, or even during a taxi ride to the location. Here's one of my secrets: when I'm really stumped, I turn to the Yellow Pages. This marvelous book is like a directory of potential "Candid Camera" gags.

Once, while thumbing through the Yellow Pages, I became intrigued with an ad for a dry cleaners. The copy boasted: "We Clean Anything." I phoned the establishment and persuaded the manager to come to my office. When he arrived, and we began recording, I informed him that I wanted to *launder* some money. He didn't even blink. He assured me that all the bills would come out "crisp and clean, just like new."

In the earliest days of "Candid Microphone," the Manhattan Yellow Pages guided us to locksmiths who would unchain my secretary from her desk. In 1990, we scoured the Yellow Pages in Stamford, Connecticut, for repairmen to fix a noisy microwave oven (when they opened it they discovered an owl roosting inside).

I once called caterers from the Yellow Pages, to help me arrange a testimonial dinner. "I'm stumped by some of the details," I told one caterer.

"Don't worry. Who's the dinner for?"

Somewhat sheepishly I told her, "It's for me."

"Fine, fine. Is it a special occasion?"

I just looked at her blankly.

"Well, have you done anything of note?"

More nervous silence.

"Don't worry, we'll either invent an occasion, or we'll say it's for all your past accomplishments."

"Okay."

"I can handle everything, the food, the hall, the decorations. All I need from you is a guest list. Can you give me a list of friends you'd like to invite?"

A long, steady pause.

"Oh, surely you must have some friends who would come!"

"No, not really."

This didn't faze her a bit; she plowed forward with the details until I told her to "Smile."

After nearly fifty years in show business, I've never had a testimonial dinner. I suppose it's good to know that if I'm ever so inclined, I can find one through the Yellow Pages.

Affairs of Art and Heart

You've never heard of him?" the art dealer asked, looking shocked. We were standing in front of a painting which I thought was the oddest piece of art I'd ever seen. Still, the dealer showing the painting was extremely proud of it.

"What's his name again?" I asked.

"Sir Lawrence Alma-Tadema."

"Never heard of him," I said. "And furthermore, I was a student of art history so I should know the great painters."

"This *is* one of the greats," the dealer explained. "But he's distinguished in a rather unusual way. He's known as the world's worst painter."

I went home and pulled out my art encyclopedia and, sure enough, there was an article referring to Sir Lawrence Alma-Tadema as "reputedly the worst painter of the 19th century." Now there's a bold statement. First of all, how did they know there was a "worst"? Did someone survey the works of all artists in the whole world? And, secondly, the painting I saw, while different, was, in a strange way, fascinating.

Like a detective on a hot case, I spent all my spare moments away from "Candid Camera" investigating the life and paintings of this Sir Lawrence Alma-Tadema.

I learned that he was English and had lived from 1836 to 1912, enjoying enormous popularity in his day. His house in London, which I eventually visited, was full of furniture he designed himself, and his paintings were hung in frames he designed and built. He was enormously prolific and, as a result, developed an "opus" numbering system to prevent copies of his works from being sold. However, his reputation fell off sharply after his death and, by the 1960s, he was virtually unknown.

One day while reading through some art books I made an interesting discovery. It turned out that Alma-Tadema had an affair with the wife of the art critic who branded him the world's worst painter. Apparently this damning statement, which had followed him down through the years, was not made by an objective critic but a jealous husband.

At the same time I began to be seduced by Alma-Tadema's art. He was a painter of extraordinary skill who captured Greek and Roman scenes in an unusual way. Every inch of every canvas is packed with excitement. And I found that in many paintings there is one person staring straight out of the canvas. It is a startling and intriguing device.

In short order, I began to buy as many of Alma-Tadema's paintings as I could find. Soon I had the largest collection of his paintings in the world.

I should back up a little bit and put this in the context of my life. I had gone art shopping to decorate the walls of my new apartment where I was moving with my second wife, Marilyn, whom I had met the year before.

Marilyn had been hired as a secretary on "Candid Camera" while I was on the road filming. The fellow who hired her had filled her with horror stories about how tough I was on the staff. He made her so jumpy that Marilyn tried to quit the day I first came back to the office. She ran out to the elevator, but I pursued her and talked her into staying.

How strange life is. If the elevator had arrived immediately and Marilyn had vanished, my life would be so different. But the elevator was slow, and by the time the door opened something had been exchanged between Marilyn and me which plunged us into a powerful relationship.

In the early days, Marilyn sat at a desk outside my office. She was almost twenty-five years younger than me, a nervy, Jewish woman who was a total knockout. When she crossed her gorgeous legs, any man would give her what she wanted. And soon she got it—a marriage that would last fourteen years and produce two children. But first, she wanted to try her hand at being in "Candid Camera" gags.

Marilyn never had any formal acting lessons, but I soon found she could improvise in an endearing fashion. One stunt she did on the show involved former President Harry Truman. He was known to come to New York City and walk down Park Avenue to his law offices. We arranged to have Marilyn at every street corner as he walked by. She'd call out, "Good morning, Mr. President!" Then she quickly jumped into a car, and we'd scoot her around so she could be waiting for him at the next corner.

Truman didn't notice for the first few blocks. But then he began giving her odd looks as he tried to figure out what was going on. By the sixth time he saw her, he must have figured it out. When she gave him her cheerful "Good morning, Mr.

President," he called back, "That's the last time, lady. You won't catch me again."

In another gag, we made a dress for Marilyn that was rigged in such a way that when she took a drag on a cigarette, smoke came out of every seam. She sat down next to this guy at a lunch counter and asked if he minded if she smoked. He said no, so she lit up. Soon smoke was billowing everywhere. She played it perfectly. She kept on smoking and saying, "Don't worry, this happens all the time."

Marilyn's flightiness was such a contrast to Evelyn's solid, stable personality. Our eighteen-year marriage had been so filled with my career and raising children that we scarcely noticed we had grown far apart. What had drawn me to Evelyn, in addition to her great beauty, was her poise, calm manner, and sound-as-a-dollar personality. But now that I was approaching fifty, I missed the sparks, the foolishness of a real love affair. I sensed that this was my last chance to make a move before life closed in on me. Soon I rented a Park Avenue apartment and spent many nights with Marilyn in the city while Evelyn stayed with the kids at our estate at Croton-on-Hudson.

When I announced that I wanted a divorce, Evelyn accepted the news calmly. She even agreed to my suggestion that Marilyn and I live near the family in another building on our estate. It was my lofty hope that we could make a smooth transition so that Evelyn and the children would get to know Marilyn. I wanted them to know I didn't hate anyone. I wasn't angry. I thought if we could all eat around the same table, they could eventually accept each other.

That arrangement lasted about a year, until Marilyn grew restless for her own place. We did some shopping and found a gorgeous corner duplex in Manhattan on the eleventh floor of the Beresford overlooking Central Park. It was possibly the best location in all of New York. One side faced the park and the other side faced the planetarium and the Museum of Natural History. Among our neighbors were the violinist Itzhak Perlman and the film director Mike Nichols.

Soon I was involved in remodeling this wonderful space and decorating it in a unique way. We made the living room Victorian, the library Chinese, the bedroom Spanish. But everyone agreed that the kitchen and bathrooms were the most interesting. In fact, when the word got out about what we had done, *The New York Times* did a feature article on the apartment. Here's what the writer liked best:

> The his-and-her's bathrooms off the master bedroom are two of the apartment's high points. His has, in addition to the special shaving mirror and the aquarium, a television set, hi-fi, a whirl-pool bath and a sauna. Hers has a bidet, professional hairdryer, and such a pleasant view of Central Park that Mrs. Funt uses the bathroom as her office.
>
> But the Funt family favorite is the kitchen. An enormous room with dark carved-wood paneling, it features a dining and utility table, each mounted on barber chair bases; stained glass skylights; and two ovens, two stoves, two refrigerators and two freezers.
>
> "I've always lived in homes where things break down," Mr. Funt explained. "When you have two of everything, one is bound to work."

The walls in this apartment were like those of a museum. The place was built on a grand scale, and its architecture deserved the best classic paintings. And that's what brought me to the art gallery that afternoon. I was innocently looking for a way to decorate an apartment. What I stumbled across was an all-consuming passion that continued for years. Soon, our walls were covered with Alma-Tadema canvases depicting riotous orgies in ancient Rome, parades through the streets of Athens, and Anthony and Cleopatra gliding down the Nile.

In the art field, if someone is collecting a certain painter, there is a ripple that spreads through the entire community. Soon, word got out that Allen Funt was collecting the paintings of Alma-Tadema, and the prices of his paintings started to rise.

At this point, one of Alma-Tadema's paintings came on the market at the Parke Bernet gallery in Los Angeles. It showed at least 100 women with rapturous expressions parading through the streets of Athens.

I decided I had to have this painting.

The dealer said, "This is an absolute gem. If you want to buy it, you have to decide in advance how much you're willing to bid." After a moment she added, "It would be best if you don't come to the auction in person. If they see you, it'll make it too expensive. You can bid by phone."

I queried all my art dealer friends about what I should pay for this painting. The consensus was I shouldn't pay any more than $25,000.

On the day of the auction, I was sitting in my kitchen alone waiting for Parke Bernet to call. Finally, the phone rang and the dealer on the other end said they had opened the bidding for "Spring."

The bidding started very high, at about $15,000. Right away I knew I was in deep water.

Before I knew it, the price was up around $18,000 and climbing. Nineteen, twenty. Someone wanted the painting as badly as I did. The price kept going up—twenty-three, twenty-five. In no time at all, we were into the thirties.

Finally I caught myself and told the dealer, "I don't want it that badly. I pass."

The dealer said, "Don't go away. I want to find out who bought it." A moment later she said, "Allen, don't be disappointed; at least you lost to a good opponent."

"Who was it?"

"The Getty Museum," she said. "And I think they're mad at you. You made them pay about $15,000 more than they planned. If it wasn't for your bidding, they would have gotten that painting for nothing."

Living in that amazing Beresford apartment, surrounded by so many extraordinary Alma-Tadema paintings, was an experience I'll always cherish. It was as if every inch of every canvas was singing to me. I felt I could spend days in front of a single painting and still see things I never noticed before.

So many unusual things happened with that collection of paintings. One night I was asleep in my room when I was awakened by a loud crash. I ran to the living room and found that a beautiful Alma-Tadema painting had fallen (the wire which held it up had snapped) and landed so that the canvas was pierced right through the face of the leading lady.

I had paid $30,000 for the painting so I was determined to have it restored. I found an expert who was himself a highly accomplished painter. He said he could weave the canvas back together and repaint the face to match the original. But after about a week, he called me and said, "I'm having a real problem. In order to restore it, I had to take off a little paint around the tear. And I found that there is another painting below it. And there is another painting below that. Now I don't know how to paint the face that was torn."

I decided that I would take photographs of the faces on dozens of Alma-Tadema canvases and let him make a composite. When the restorer finished the painting, I felt the face was subtly different than the other paintings. But that didn't harm its value, as you'll shortly see. But first, there's one last twist in the Alma-Tadema story which I have to relate.

One day a neighbor of ours in the Beresford came by and asked to see my collection. He explained that he was a curator at the Metropolitan Museum where they were beginning a series of exhibitions of private collections. He asked if he could display my Alma-Tadema paintings and in return, loan me paintings for the same insured value. He invited me to come to the museum and see some of the paintings that I might borrow.

When I arrived, I was amazed at the paintings they were offering: El Grecos, Rembrandts—paintings by the masters of the world. What I didn't realize then was that they were actually "from the school of." In other words, they were done by other painters but were still extremely valuable.

Soon after I had these classic paintings at home, *The New York Times* art department called and asked if they could write a piece about the exchange. Unbeknownst to me, this critic was having a running battle with the curator for the Metropolitan Museum. When the article came out in the *Times*, it said something like, "'Candid Camera' trickster collects a house full of masterpieces in exchange for the paintings of the worst painter of the 19th Century." The article created a lot of interest in my Alma-Tadema collection, which, as it turned out, would soon be critical to my livelihood.

In the early seventies, I lost all my money.

The reason for my financial crisis is a story and a chapter in itself that I'll cover later. For now I'll just say that I was, for a time, reduced to zero. The only thing I could do to stay solvent was to sell my Alma-Tadema paintings. It almost broke my heart to think of losing them, but I finally called Parke Bernet and arranged for an auction.

The dealer I contacted said, "These paintings are gold; we can sell them for you in one of two ways. Either you ask us to guarantee you a price as the bottom line, or you wait for the auction and take whatever the bidding brings."

I thought about it briefly and said, "In my particular situation, I have to get the guaranteed price."

Before they carted off my precious paintings, I had the foresight to hire one of the best art photographers in New York to take pictures of all the canvases. I also kept back a few of Alma-Tadema's frames and now have those photographs hanging in the original frames in my house. But the real paintings were shipped off to England and auctioned there. They sold for fabulous prices—many times more than what I paid for them. And the highest price was paid for the one which had been repainted by the art restorer as a composite of all of Alma-Tadema's women.

Now that my fortunes have returned, people ask why I don't track down and buy back those Alma-Tadema paintings. First of all, the paintings have scattered all over the world—from Germany to Japan. But also, I think it's futile to try to recapture something you once loved. I already had my love affair with those wonderful paintings. You just can't go back to Niagara Falls and see it again for the first time.

Keep on Smiling

SOMETIMES I wish I had never invented one of TV's most famous slogans. It's a strange claim to fame that "Smile! You're on 'Candid Camera'" appears in more toilets throughout the world than any other piece of graffiti.

Cops love to pull me over even when I'm driving perfectly, just for the fun of saying, "Smile, Allen. You're on Candid Radar!" When I lost my money to an embezzler, tabloids 'round the world used the headline: SMILE, YOU'RE BROKE.

Cartoonists have had a ball with our slogan. My wall is covered with cartoons depicting bank holdups, cheating husbands, even reconnaissance satellites—all captioned with our trademark phrase. And I've seen quite a few convenience stores with security cameras and a warning, "Smile, you may be on 'Candid Camera.'"

I can't even say for sure how I stumbled upon the smile slogan. In the early days, Al Slep of our staff coined several phrases that I used as sign-offs. For instance: "Until next time, you go your way and we'll go your way too, with the 'Candid Camera!'" Al also wrote that the people we photographed were "caught in the act of being themselves."

We often quoted, with modernization, from the poet Robert Burns: "O wad some power the giftie gie us, to see oursels as others see us." I have that passage framed in my office, with Burns' autograph, dated 1788.

It wasn't until 1961 that I first said, "Smile! You're on 'Candid Camera'" on CBS. Within months, a grateful mother wrote to me about an incident involving her teenage daughter.

She was riding home late at night on the New York City subway when she was confronted by two rough-looking characters. She couldn't explain why, but in a moment of panic she blurted out, "Smile, boys, you're on 'Candid Camera,'" and they ran quickly out of the car.

Cast and Characters

I was in my office one afternoon when my receptionist burst in. "There's a woman in the lobby who's asked to see you," she said. "And I really think I should bring her in."

People walked in off the street all the time asking to see me, and my receptionist was very good at getting rid of them. I was curious to know why this one was different.

A moment later a rather ordinary-looking middle-aged woman was standing in front of my desk. She was nervous but very determined.

"Mr. Funt," she began. "I think I have the greatest stunt for you."

Many people thought that. Few actually had any idea of what made a good "Candid Camera" gag. But I told her to continue.

"You see, I have a pet monkey that I've trained to sit on top of my head. No matter where I go or what I do, this monkey will calmly sit on my head. You ought to be able to figure out some way to use it on your show."

It did indeed seem like something we could use. And the way she presented it to me seemed like a challenge. But I had no idea that it would, in some ways, become the perfect "Candid Camera" sequence.

"Thanks," I said. "I'll be in touch."

A week later we began filming this setup. We hired an employment counselor to screen secretarial applicants. His "job" was to interview people and provide a rough idea of their personality, appearance and skills.

We sent in two or three women from our staff to get him going, then we sent in Fannie Flagg as an applicant. She was perfect for the job. You could see the employment counselor warming up to her and getting ready to recommend we hire her.

But at the end of the interview, Fannie said to him, "There is one thing I have to tell you. Everywhere I go, there's a lady following me with a monkey on her head. I'll probably see her later today."

You could immediately see by the employment counselor's expression that he discarded this candidate. "Thank you," he said and showed her to the door.

Twenty seconds went by and in came the woman with the monkey sitting on her head. She mumbled something, then rushed out.

The employment counselor's face dropped.

Moments later Fannie returned. "I've been thinking," she explained. "I know that I'm imagining this woman, and I'm going to see a doctor."

Now this guy was in a real bind. Should he tell her or not? After looking at her for a long time he asked, "What's the name of your doctor?"

"Why?" asked Fannie. "Aren't you feeling well?"

"I feel fine. I just want to see how you're doing."

Fannie Flagg, who went on to write the book and movie *Fried Green Tomatoes*, was one of our most skilled performers. We used her because she had a knack for fitting into many different roles, while at the same time being herself—a combination that is hard to find.

To demonstrate what I mean, consider another scene in which a man was told to deliver a package to an office where Fannie was working. When he arrived, her back was to him. But then she turned and he could see that she had a beard—not a full beard, but sort of a goatee. Still, he was all business, asking her to sign for the package. She made up an excuse and left the room.

Then we sent in another "Candid Camera" performer, who asked the deliveryman where the other woman had gone. The deliveryman answered, "Oh, you mean the bearded lady?"

"What? She had a few whiskers or something?"

"Oh no," the deliveryman said, "a full beard. It was a real beaut."

At this point Fannie reappeared and said, "Excuse me, but was someone in here talking about my beard? Because I'm really self-conscious about it."

This guy was completely unfazed by being challenged. "No," he said. "*Beer*. I said I could go for a beer."

It took a special talent to pull off a scene like this because Fannie had to be normal in every way, except for the beard. The absurdity of the situation—acting as if nothing was out of the ordinary—was what made it funny.

Finding guest stars for "Candid Camera" was always a challenge. We wanted names the public would recognize (our guiding principle was whether *TV Guide* might find them worth mentioning in its listing), but we didn't want people who were identified with a single character. For example, we used Phil

Silvers, although to the public he had become the character of Sergeant Bilko from his TV show.

Part of the problem with big-name guests is that most secretly hoped to be recognized while working "undercover" on "Candid Camera." But two popular fellows, who left their egos behind when they came to work for us on a golf course in New Jersey, were Mickey Mantle and Yogi Berra. It was 1962, and Mantle had just won the Most Valuable Player award for the third time. Yet, dressed in tattered clothing, posing as caddies, he and Yogi went unrecognized. They did all the things caddies should avoid—talking too much, sneezing as their clients started to swing, and giving bad advice. One golfer was so exasperated, he allowed Mickey to tee one up and drive it, just to keep him quiet. The damn thing went about 350 yards.

Certain guests really couldn't be disguised, even if we had placed bags over their heads. I'm thinking of Jayne Mansfield, who worked for us in '61, and Dolly Parton, who made her appearance in '75. I decided to allow both of these beauties to simply play themselves.

Jayne hailed cabs outside a hotel in New Orleans. She told the cabbies that her beloved poodle needed a ride to the airport. No problem. But the poodle wouldn't cooperate unless carried inside the drivers' shirts, close to the chest, as Jayne was happy to demonstrate. Every cabbie was accommodating.

Dolly, too, found men were eager to help as she stood in a huge parking lot with a bandage on her left ankle. She persuaded male passersby to carry her to her car, a white convertible. Of course, we made certain that there were five identical white convertibles in that lot. Most guys seemed on the verge of collapse by the time they reached the fifth car, but they all seemed to enjoy it.

Over the years I also realized that actors slightly past their professional prime, whose names everyone still knew, were the best for us. Their phones weren't ringing, and they wanted to work. Dorothy Lamour was featured in the famous split car, and Audrey Meadows, who had just come off "The Jackie Gleason Show," talked a tax collector into using public money to play the ponies. Later we used Wally Cox in a piece where he taught birdcalls to New Jersey longshoremen.

One such actor who was especially good on "Candid Camera" was the immortal Buster Keaton. His career was in a lull at that time, but he was just as funny as ever—the kind of performer you could turn loose without much direction and who would spontaneously create a routine.

Buster did a marvelous sequence at a lunch counter. It was nothing more than a series of spills and calamities, all of which were witnessed by a young couple sitting next to him. They couldn't help watching (out of the corners of their eyes), but they didn't want to laugh openly at this poor old man with the long, sad face.

Finally, with a big bowl of soup in front of him, Buster pretended to sneeze. The sneeze was so violent that his toupee fell into the soup. When this happened, the young couple almost fell off their stools laughing, yet all the time trying to contain themselves. I've found there is nothing more laugh-provoking than watching people try *not* to laugh.

Another legend we used on "Candid Camera" was Harpo Marx. The challenge was to find a way to use him without, of course, having him say a word. We wound up putting him inside a Coke machine. When someone put in a coin, Harpo would go into action, mixing the drink by hand, clowning away, and occasionally honking his trademark horn. Most people couldn't figure out what he was doing and would stand there, transfixed, as he went through an elaborate pantomime. I did learn, though, that Harpo was always true to his screen persona and never said a word.

Silence was not Jonathan Winters' trademark. In fact, his best moments were when the words were in such a race to get out of his mouth that he had to resort to sound effects. Before we used Jonathan, I wondered if he was so far out that no one would believe him.

We had Jonathan drive up to a tollbooth and report to the attendant that he had just seen a spaceship landing in New Jersey. At first the attendant looked at Jonathan like he was out of his mind. But as Jonathan continued with his description of the encounter with the little people on the space ship, enhancing it with sound effects, the attendant began to buy into his story. His expression seemed to say, "Either we put this guy in the booby hatch, or I better run before those little people from the flying saucer come this way."

Over the years of working with actors and actresses on "Candid Camera" we devised three Golden Rules we told all our performers:

1. Keep your back to the camera. This is nearly impossible for most actors since it violates every rule they have been taught. But the audience must focus on the subject, not the actor.

2. Listen. To many actors trained in improvisation, silence is a sin. But on "Candid Camera," the pauses often provide the most dramatic moments. You can almost feel the other person thinking, "What on earth am I going to do?"

3. Let the other person be funny. Actors are very competitive. They have to be ready with a good line whenever they find an opening. On our show, they have to squelch this tendency and let themselves be topped by the other person.

Besides older actors, we occasionally took a chance during the sixties on up-and-coming talents such as Charles Grodin and Carol Burnett. While these performers were funny when they were in character, they weren't very comfortable being themselves. An exception was Woody Allen.

Someone on our staff had seen Woody's stand-up routine in a nightclub and loved it, so we asked him to come talk to us. I'd like to think that the visibility on "Candid Camera" helped his career. But the truth is he was already moving fast and was destined to be a big star.

Woody was funny in everything he did for us. His best piece involved dictating a love letter to a stenographer. Of course, it was a completely ridiculous love letter. And to allow the stenographer to react to the situation, Woody turned his back to her. His dictation went something like this:

"I love you... Exclamation point. I must have you...Two exclamation points. The world revolves around you... Question mark."

The best stenographer we filmed was a tough, gum chewing, wisecracking Brooklyn type wearing glasses with rhinestones in the corners. Finally, Woody asked her to read the letter back. After each phrase, such as, "'I must have you'—two exclamation points," she rolled her eyes and stifled her laughter.

The scene ended when Woody told her, "Take another letter. Address this one to Allen Funt."

The stenographer started writing, then stopped. "Hey, wait a second," she stammered, looking around the room as her wisecracking attitude dissolved into a look of almost innocent vulnerability. "You finally caught me," she said, breaking into laughter.

I've often heard that Woody Allen tightly controls the use of his material on television. However, we recently needed to get permission to use a "Candid Camera" piece of his. It was right in the midst of all his troubles with Mia Farrow. But the answer came back quickly, "No problem, go ahead and use it."

There was another major comic who got her start on "Candid Camera." Unfortunately I'm prohibited from naming her as the result of a lawsuit. The suit was so ridiculous, it could have only happened to me.

When I first interviewed this comic, she seemed lively and funny. But when we tried to use her on the show, she was terrible. She wouldn't keep quiet. Furthermore, everything she did had a smutty tinge to it. This same off-color humor served her well later as a comic and talk show host, but it made it difficult to use her material on "Candid Camera."

At that time, it was my habit to take a sauna late in the day to help me unwind. I would then meet with the writers and other staff members wearing my bathrobe. In this comic's autobiography, published a few years ago, she claimed I "exposed" myself to her during one of these meetings.

Her allegation wasn't true at all, and she knew it.

Through her lawyer, who happened to be mine too, I said, "Can we settle?"

He said yes, and we reached a unique settlement which I'll explain in a later chapter.

In some cases, the performers we used on "Candid Camera" weren't actors at all—and they came to us in unexpected ways. One day I was sitting in my car in front of the office waiting for my secretary to bring me some papers. All of a sudden, a big smiling face appeared in my car window and said, "You want me to be on your show?" It took me a couple of seconds to recover my poise and recognize that this was Muhammad Ali.

Muhammad had just won a fight where he had earned about $3 million for a minute in the ring. So when it came time to discuss his fee, I thought I'd appeal to him in the same way— but for smaller stakes. I said, "I'll pay you a thousand dollars a minute." He said, "Okay, but there has to be a minimum of fifteen minutes."

As I got to know Muhammad, I found that he knew all the different roles people wanted him to play: the braggart, the champ, the charmer. He'd even make up bits of poetry which he would recite. He was magnetic, bright, and seemed fascinated by life.

One of the most exciting evenings I had was when Muhammad and his wife came to our home at the Beresford. They spent hours admiring my Alma-Tadema paintings, and, when he came to one painting in particular, he stopped, captivated. It was an Egyptian scene involving the baby Moses. In the background were several slaves, painted as strong, beautiful, proud people. That really grabbed him. He wanted to buy that painting from me in the worst way, but I just couldn't part with it.

Meanwhile, the challenge was to use Muhammad on "Candid Camera" in such a way that he could be himself, yet not be recognized. He did several pieces for us, the best involving a class of eight-year-olds who were given an assignment to write a composition called "If I could meet Muhammad Ali, this is what I'd tell him." While the kids were writing, Muhammad was actually in the room, dressed in custodian's coveralls, cleaning the blackboards.

One kid wrote, "I don't like Muhammad Ali. If I could see him I'd tell him I don't like him. But my sister is crazy about him." When the assignments were collected, Muhammad stripped off his coveralls, and there stood the champ in his boxing shorts. He pounded his chest and confronted this kid about what he'd written. The only thing the boy could say was, "You want to meet my sister?"

It would be misleading to suggest that all "Candid Camera" performers were on the star level of Woody Allen or

Muhammad Ali. We had a stable of wonderfully gifted actors who remained relatively unknown. Usually, these actors had a specialty that was useful for our show.

We had a guy on our staff named Joey Faye who was a good utility player. He could do anything—including sneezing at will. It was amazing how many gags we worked around Joey's sneeze. The best was this: we rang the number of a public phone until someone answered it (there's always someone who will pick up a public phone if it rings enough). So along came this battleax of a woman who answered the phone. On the other end Joey pretended that he was lost and needed directions to City Hall. But he had a nasty cold. We rigged the public phone so that whenever Joey sneezed, water sprayed out of the receiver and squirted the woman in the face. What was wonderful about it was that it never occurred to her that it was mechanically impossible for this to happen. After several squirts, she told Joey, "I'm going to break every bone in your body!"

In addition to Joey Faye, our roster of "Candid" players included talented ad-libbers such as Ben Joelson, Bob Schwartz, Marge Green, and Tom O'Malley. Tom often got the toughest assignments because of his skill in what I call "nervy" bits. Tom could push a shopping cart through the aisles of a supermarket and casually pluck groceries from the carts of other shoppers. That was nervy. Once he played a restaurant busboy who was so nervy he whisked away customers' plates before they had finished eating. That stunt provided an unexpected twist when one of the diners recognized Tom as an old friend. She didn't mind losing her unfinished meal, but she nearly collapsed over the discovery that Tom was so destitute that he needed to work as a busboy.

We also did a series of "crying" gags that centered on how men react to women in tears. It started with the actress Betsy Palmer who could cry on cue. She played a dentist who was nervous because it was her first day and everything was going wrong. She pretended to get flustered and began *shaving* the guy in the chair. It was a wild scene. But on her own, she decided the climax was for her to start crying. It was effective because instead of the guy being angry, he shifted the emphasis to consoling her.

Almost thirty years later we tried a similar piece in which Victoria Jackson of "Saturday Night Live" played a doctor on her first day. Sure enough, when Victoria's tears started to flow, the subjects melted—the *male* subjects, that is. A female patient scolded this "doctor" so harshly that we were afraid she might grab a scalpel and end Victoria's career on the spot.

Besides hiring guest performers for the show, I also had to make sure I hired the best possible cohost. After all the feuding I'd had with Arthur Godfrey, I wanted someone who would bring a sense of harmony to the set. After a long interview process, Durwood Kirby, who had been a regular on "The Garry Moore Show," was my choice. He stayed with us for five years, from 1961 to 1966, and his name became closely linked with "Candid Camera."

Durwood was good for our show because he had average looks and demeanor, while being almost Lincolnesque in his bearing. He was a versatile actor, but we used him most for man-on-the-street type interviews. He could stop people and ask the most outlandish questions, such as, what's a good excuse I can give my wife to explain my not coming home last night? Somehow the normalcy of his looks offset the outrageousness of the request.

I also began to use Durwood to help me test pieces. It seemed that his taste was about the same as that of America's television audience. I felt that if Durwood understood a gag, and enjoyed it, America would get it. So he became part of my test group along with that tollbooth operator and the studio orchestra. I'm not sure why we ever stopped using Durwood. But the next cohost we had was as flamboyant as Durwood was stable.

Bess Myerson, the former Miss America, joined us in 1966. The fact that she was Jewish, beautiful and brilliant made it a challenge to get her on the show. It's always been my opinion that brilliant women have an especially difficult time in life. This is because society, particularly back then, encouraged them to hide their true abilities so men didn't feel threatened. And this was Bess's problem.

Like Arthur Godfrey, whose performance was affected by cancer treatments, Bess was challenged by her tempestuous off-camera life. She was going through a difficult divorce with her husband, Arnold Grant, a prominent Manhattan attorney. She had lived most of her life under the shadow of this man and was now trying to break free.

Bess only lasted a year on our show, but it was a very rewarding year for me, giving birth to a friendship that endures to this day. Afterward she entered politics and held a high position in New York City government close to Mayor Ed Koch.

While we were producing "Candid Camera" for syndication in the mid-seventies, I turned to another former Miss America to be cohost, Phyllis George. Phyllis was an effervescent addition to our series, and since our tapings had been moved from New York to Nashville, her Southern charm fit perfectly. But on one occasion, Phyllis missed her plane to Nashville and decided to skip the taping entirely. I phoned her agent and called Phyllis some names I never should have uttered. That was the last we saw of Phyllis George.

It has probably become clear by now that "Candid Camera" was a revolving door of creative people—performers, writers, and producers. Some of this may have had to do with my own off-camera personality, which could be very abrasive at times. I didn't think about it much in the early years; it just seemed that someone had to take a strong stand to keep the show on track. After all, television production is a hectic, high-pressure environment. There is no place for weakness and indecision.

But lately I've become more reflective about my behavior. What brought it to mind was a conversation I had recently with my former wife, Marilyn, who started as a secretary on the show. She had been very depressed. So when she began dating someone new, I hoped it would pick up her spirits. One day on the telephone, I innocently asked how the relationship was going.

"Fine," was her curt response.

"Well, is he a good friend?" I continued.

"What do you mean?" she asked.

"Well, for example, are you sleeping with him?"

"What's the matter with you?" she said. "I would never tell you that."

"But Marilyn, I tell you everything. There haven't been many since you, but I've told you about them all. So why are you hesitating?"

There was a long pause. Finally, she said, "If I told you I was sleeping with him, you'd be on the next plane to New York to find out who he was so you could break his legs."

I was dumbfounded. "Marilyn. That's not me at all."

"You may have an image of what you're like. But mine is this: you have always scared the living daylights out of everyone, including me. "

"On the show too?"

"Especially on the show. You got angry. And when you got angry, you got menacing. And that's the way you were in the office."

"Marilyn," I said, "are you sure?"

"Absolutely."

You have to bear in mind that Marilyn is easily frightened. Still, I couldn't completely shake the things she said. It is true that I have always had little patience with slow thinkers; but my greatest wrath is reserved for cowards and liars. If I sent someone off to film a piece, and he came back full of excuses about why it didn't work or what went wrong, and took no blame himself, then I'd chew that guy up.

To some degree, this dictatorial personality came with the role of top producer. I've heard that Milton Berle was very explosive on his show. And even a guy as benign as Red Skelton was a terror on the set.

But while some creative people came and went, we had a core of loyal staff people at "Candid Camera," who were never reticent about speaking their minds. I was particularly fond of Ann Richardson, a producer; Martin Rich, an editor; and Pat Terzini, an assistant camera operator, who were not the least bit afraid of me. And this caused me to value their opinions enormously.

Pat was a straightforward guy. When we screened a sequence for an upcoming show, there might be ten others in the room—all quiet, waiting to let someone else to express an opinion first. But if Pat didn't like it, he didn't hesitate for a second—he'd give it the thumbs down. He was the viewer I was aiming for, the type of person who had an immediate reaction to what he saw.

Pat was the opposite of the critics and intellectuals. They might laugh at the show. But then they'd go away and think about whether it was low- or highbrow. And they'd get tied in knots wondering what I was trying to say about human nature. With that group I always seemed to come up short.

I've spent a lot of time in this chapter talking about the people who appeared on "Candid Camera" without once mentioning my favorites. I've saved them for their own chapter because they are so special to me. I'm referring to those in our society who are honest, wildly creative, and always surprising. When you turn to Chapter Eight, you'll see who I'm talking about.

The Art of Listening

OVER the years, I learned a valuable lesson: if you believe everyone has something important to say, you'll be a good listener.

Unfortunately, most people engaged in conversation are only waiting for their turn to talk. They're waiting, but they're not really listening. The only way to elicit interesting comments from people is to listen carefully to what they say and formulate leading questions. The success of my television shows depends on my ability to get people to open up and talk—to get the best out of them.

I learned this the hard way. Often, I made a judgment about someone that they were dull, until I finally fed them the right question. Then they became a different person, because they were talking about something they loved.

Good listening is almost a natural gift. But it can be learned if you develop a genuine interest in other people—and remember to keep your own mouth shut.

Candid Kids

One day as I was leaving my office, I stopped into a toy store to buy my son a birthday present. He was turning six and like many boys back in the fifties, he spent a lot of time pretending he was a cowboy. I purchased a toy gun and holster and tossed it on the car seat next to me as I began my commute to Westchester County, New York.

Soon I found myself behind a car driven by a couple with a youngster in the backseat. I looked at him and he looked at me, then I found myself looking down the barrel of his six-shooter as he began taking potshots at me. I let it pass at first, until I glanced down at the seat next to me and remembered that I was armed. How could I resist? I picked up my own gun and a shoot-out began that lasted for the next ten miles.

Just as I was drawing a final bead on this kid, his father turned around. He slammed on the brakes (naturally, I did the same), jumped out of his car, and chewed me out so long that a state trooper stopped to see what the problem was. Imagine my embarrassment in trying to explain to the cop that we were just having a friendly gunfight. And all this time the boy was innocently smiling at me from behind his father's leg.

For some reason I have always related well to kids below the age of about eight. As long as they are young, still believe in Santa Claus, are afraid of the dark, and think they could grow up to be anything in the whole world, then I'm great. But my magnetism seems to disappear when a kid reaches nine or ten. Then the golden days have passed, and I'm just another old man.

During the early days of television, there were two top entertainers known for their work with children, Danny Kaye and Art Linkletter. Danny Kaye was a wonderful clown, but he never engaged the child very much. He would make funny faces and get the child laughing, yet the emphasis was always on him.

Art Linkletter was more the deceptive type. He'd lead a youngster into a situation, winking at the camera as the child innocently said things that adults could interpret in slightly risqué ways.

I made it my business to avoid both of these approaches whenever I interacted with children on "Candid Camera."

When I first considered including children on our show, there was great resistance. Since our sponsor was the tobacco giant Philip Morris, the network felt that made the show unfit for kids. I argued that we wanted to film kids, not broadcast material *for* kids. Eventually they allowed us to try a piece, and the response was overwhelming. From then on, children became a rich source of material and one of the most popular features of the show.

By the time "Candid Camera" began its most popular run, 1960 to '68, I had three children by Evelyn, my first wife: Peter was thirteen, Patty ten, and John seven. Having children of my own gave me a handy testing ground for situations involving kids.

Still, filming kids for our show was no easy task. Try, for a moment, imagining the following scene from a six-year-old's perspective, and you'll understand the problem.

One day, your teacher suddenly takes you out of class and says, "I want you to go into the next room and talk with the new teacher." This has never happened before. Immediately you think you're in trouble. So you go to the next classroom, and there is a man about your father's age, who begins asking you questions. And you're thinking: Is this some kind of test? What have I done wrong? Am I going to miss recess?

Now let's switch back to my point of view. We have arrived at this school the night before, chosen a location, and set up our equipment. (Unlike the adults, we have to be extra careful about hiding cameras around children. They are eagle-eyed when it comes to spotting anything out of the ordinary.)

We're ready to roll, and here comes the first kid. The problem is, he's suspicious and frightened. My greeting brings a terse response. My next comment brings only a tight little shrug. How can I gain the confidence of this child?

Often, I'd bring out a book of matches and say, "Would you do me a favor Johnny? I have a problem with matches. I don't know how to blow them out. When I strike this match, will you blow it out for me?"

"Sure!" he'd say.

Then I'd light the match, and he would blow it out.

"Thanks," I'd say, as if it was an enormous relief. "I don't know why, but I've always hated to blow out matches."

That little action immediately changed our relationship. The child knew I didn't look down on him, and he had found something he was better at than I.

In other cases, I relaxed children by asking them to help me with things that really were bothering me. I might say, "Johnny, I'm so miserable about this bald head of mine. What should I do about it?" Or, I'd say, "I feel like I'm getting old." Whatever problems I had on my mind, I'd take them to the children. And while their answers were often inspiring, they also broke the ice between us.

But even these techniques failed when we were filming Eskimo children in Alaska. An old woman who was watching came to my rescue. She waved me over and said two words, "Chewing gum."

"What do you mean, chewing gum?" I asked.

"These children will do anything for chewing gum."

I sent someone out for a dozen packs. As soon as the kids saw that gum, their personalities seemed to change. We got a nice sequence of their little faces peeking in the door, hoping to get a stick of gum from this strange man from a far-off place.

Over the years with "Candid Camera," I must have visited hundreds of schools across the country and talked to thousands of children. We discussed just about every subject imaginable, from love, marriage, families and other kids; to school, grown-ups, Santa Claus and astronauts. We photographed kids as they went through the significant new experiences of life, from tying their shoes, to learning the alphabet; from sharing candy, to getting their first haircut. Those memories are some of the warmest I have because they showed me what a wonderful, magical state children live in. If we could all revisit that state of mind once a week, we would be healthier adults and the world would be a better place.

One thing I really admire about children is their willingness to take on a new role and play it for all it's worth. It seems they aren't completely sure who they are yet, so they are eager to try out new personalities. Susan, a four-and-a-half year old from New Rochelle, New York, easily flipped back and forth between being her mother and herself. But, as the scene progressed, the two personalities inevitably clashed.

We sat across a table with toy phones between us. I told her to pretend she was her mother, Joyce, calling her father, Morty, at work. She asked him to buy some food on the way home. As Morty, I was agreeable, but at the end of the conversation I told her she shouldn't call me back, "unless you have a serious problem."

After I put down the phone, I spoke across the table to Susan. "Now, I'm going to keep on doing my work, and if you need anything special, you call me."

She nodded and waited, wrinkling her brow, pursing her lips, and narrowing her eyes. Finally she grabbed the phone and began to dial. Then she stopped.

"Excuse me," she whispered across the table. "I forgot the number." I whispered back some number and she dialed, making a ringing noise with her mouth.

"Listen, Mort," she said. "I have a serious problem. The children. They won't listen to me...they spill their things... they throw everything on the floor."

"Should I come home and spank them?" I asked.

"Well..." she said hesitantly as the struggle began between the Susan side of her personality and the mother side. Finally, the mother won out. "Yes."

"Which is the worst?"

"Well..." she repeated, as self-defense wrestled with the mother's objectivity. "Susan is the worst. You have to come home."

I decided to take this role playing one step further and whispered, "Pretend you're Susan now."

"Okay," she agreed, then made a condition. "But I'm only *pretending*. Then I'm the wife again."

"Susan? I got a very bad call about you, Susan. I'm going to have to punish you."

Nervous laughter was the only response.

"I'm going to have to take away your toys."

She leaned across the table and urgently whispered, "Remember, I'm only *playing* Susan."

The question of spanking is always taken seriously by children. Most are surprisingly strict.

I once asked a sweet little four-year-old if she would spank her child. She answered, "No! Well, not when it's real little... not until pretty near at least... uh, one year old...'cause that's when it kinda learns to know a little better...then POW! Yeah."

I'd have to say that while children are breathtakingly honest, there is a constant struggle between reality and the desire actually to live in that world of imagination. One little boy, Jonathan, from Bayside, New York, knew everything about dinosaurs and wouldn't stop talking about them. So after he got going on this subject, I said I was surprised he knew all this since his father was a fireman. (He had told me this earlier in the conversation.)

"But he's not really a fireman," Jonathan said. "He's a kytologist, like I'm going to be." (I think to Jonathan a kytologist was someone who studies dinosaurs.)

"Jonathan, do you ever think you can fool a grown-up?"

"Uh...sometimes...maybe..."

"You told me first that your father was a fireman...then you told me he was a 'kytologist.'"

"*That's* the real one..."

"But I understand—man to man, Jonathan—that he works in a supermarket. He's a store manager."

"Oh," he said, looking at me with a betrayed expression on his face. "You know that he's a store manager? You *know?*"

I tried to soften the blow. "Jonathan, may I tell you something? It's lovely to have those ideas about fossils and 'kytologists' and everything—but isn't it nice to have a father who is a store manager?"

He smiled and proclaimed, "Well, yes it is."

I met another boy once who was living a fantasy—but I never had a chance to point this out to him. We were doing a "Candid Camera" piece in which I was an ice cream salesman. I can't remember the exact gag. Maybe the ice cream melted too fast. Or the Popsicles fell off the stick. The problem was no one was buying ice cream, so whatever trap was planned was not being sprung. I wondered whether the lack of sales had something to do with the little boy standing nearby cradling a cat in his arms.

"Whose cat is that?" I said, looking for a way to shoo him away.

"Mine," he said. Then, sadly, he added, "I wish I could keep her."

I sensed a possible alternative sequence, so I continued. "I thought the cat was yours?"

"I wish I could keep her," he repeated, and his shoulders began shaking.

"What's the matter? Is your mother making you give it away?"

"Yes, it's scratching me all over."

By now the tears were flowing. He buried his face in the cat's fur. "I have to give it away."

"When?"

"To—" the sobbing increased, "—day."

I crouched down next to him. "Do you think, maybe, if we talked to your mother, she might let you—"

That's all it took. He happily ran off to get his mother. And we waited, hoping to film the second act to this drama. But he never returned.

Several days later we went to the address he'd given us. When his mother answered the door, I began my prepared arguments for the boy and his cat. But before I got very far, she interrupted me with her laughter. Apparently this was an old story to her. They'd had the cat for years, and it never scratched anyone. Her son did not have to get rid of the cat. She concluded that he played this game on strangers "because he wants to see what people will do."

We showed the kid and the cat on "Candid Camera," and I added the story of my visit with his mother. The sequence was well received, but every once in a while I get a funny feeling that somewhere there is a kid with a program of his own, showing *his* favorite sequences. He begins by announcing, "Now, here's one featuring an ice-cream salesman..."

Despite the fact that on CBS our show was televised at 10 p.m. and our content was aimed at adult audiences, by 1962 more than 15 percent of the "Candid Camera" viewer mail came from children. That was the year I turned to my nine-year-old son John to head our Junior Fan Mail Division. I had been in the habit of bringing home thick folders of mail on weekends, and John took an interest in reading the letters from youngsters. I had stationary printed, identifying John as the division's supervisor. He handled questions such as: What was Allen's favorite poem as a child? ("Gunga Din"); and, Why don't you create a *Candy* Camera? (We did, and it was awarded on the show to the best "Candid Kids.")

As I met and filmed children around the world, I often projected what kind of success they would have in the life ahead of them. This led to several sequences which examined the role of a child's self-image.

Once we told youngsters, "We're looking for a special kind of a child. I'd like him to be about your age. And I want him to be very smart and very strong. And nice to people." You watch a kid's face as he hears this and finally he'll say, "Oh, you must mean Dominic." Or, "You're looking for Andrew." But if you ask this question to enough children, eventually one kid comes along who gets a light in his eyes and says, "What about me?" Now that kid is going places. Somebody helped him feel that he was really special.

My countless hours in nursery schools and kindergarten classrooms helped me to see the enormous benefit that children receive from an early preschool environment. In April, 1963, I created a nonprofit foundation, dedicated to giving more kids this opportunity. We sent the following letter to several dozen schools:

As a result of our work for the "Candid Camera" television show, we have become more interested in pre-kindergarten children, their guidance and development. To that end we have established a fund providing free tuition scholarships for children of nursery school age. We invite your school to participate.

There is absolutely no obligation of any kind by the school. However, there are certain considerations which we think are important:

1. We wish the scholarship would be granted on the basis of a number of considerations of which the need of the pupil is only one.

2. We hope that on occasion children will serve to stimulate the rest of the student group by virtue of their special background.

3. We hope that in certain cases the slightly below-average child will be allowed to attend a nursery school

where he can gain the benefits of the school without creating a larger problem for the rest of the student body.

4. We trust there will be absolutely no publicity about the source of this grant and that you will in no way exploit your selection for commercial purposes.

The following September, fourteen youngsters at nine nursery schools became the first participants in our program. The selection of the children, as outlined in letters to our office, was, itself, heartwarming. For example:

Shelly is a three-and-a-half year-old girl who visits with us every day. Her mother is employed by the transportation service that our children use. She has made several friends while riding back and forth on each trip. It is not possible to explain to her why she must leave her friends and not join them in school.

Shelly's mother works two jobs for a total of 11 hours a day. It is virtually impossible for her to afford the tuition...

And:

Marshall is in desperate need of help. We believe his slow development is because of maltreatment, not retardation. Through your generosity and kindness we are able to open a door to this unwanted little fellow...

I'm happy to report that most of our students fared well in nursery school. As to my foundation, it later shifted focus and created fellowships for black students in television and radio at Syracuse University.

While my thoughts were frequently devoted to helping young people overcome serious obstacles, most of what we did on "Candid Camera" showed the humorous—or at least poignant—side of childhood. But not always. There was a darker side I occasionally observed.

The same children who were perceptive enough to spot a microphone sticking out of a flowerpot, noticed more about the world around them than they admitted to most adults. I heard about parents who screamed, fought endlessly, or never played with their children. I learned of how mothers looked when they woke up in the morning or how their fathers acted during drunken rages.

One boy told me he was an orphan—but made me promise not to tell the man and woman who adopted him that he knew. He didn't want them to feel bad, he said. Another boy told me that he knew his father was in a penitentiary, although he played a game with his mother and accepted her explanation that his father was away on a long business trip. If she knew that he knew, he whispered to me, it might make her cry.

In one case I was stunned by a little girl's revelation. She began her story by saying, "My father and I were fishing together..." I leaned forward, sensing a pleasant story about a sunny vacation.

"He hooked a big fish," she continued, her voice filled with excitement. "And then he fell off the boat." It was unexpected; this was shaping up as a good sequence. Then she added, "And he was drowned."

I sat there silently, unable to interrupt as she rushed ahead with the story. The details were still vivid to her, and their terrifying effects were painfully obvious. I eventually recovered and switched the subject back to school, her favorite games, and other children. She was charming and amusing and we got a good "Candid Camera" conversation. But that earlier part of the tape was erased and given back permanently to the silence it deserved.

It was times like this that made me appreciate the protected world most other children lived in, the one where the imagination was stronger than reality. There was one little boy in particular who showed me how clearly he could visualize an exciting future, despite the rather skimpy current evidence of its actual approach.

I met David at the Henry Street Settlement House on New York's lower East Side. We were drawn there by a music teacher who lured us with stories about his young pupils. David had been scheduled for three violin lessons. For the first, he came without a violin because his mother hadn't bought it yet; at the second, his teacher told him about the "E" and "G" strings. His third lesson was canceled because his teacher had a cold.

Now, David came into the room to tell me about his music career. I asked him how he had happened to choose the violin, and he explained that he had tried the accordion but it was too heavy.

I put my hand on his shoulder. "David, would you like to look into the future?" He nodded eagerly.

I went on to transport him to a scene twenty years ahead. He had mastered the violin. It was time for his first solo recital at Carnegie Hall.

"The audience fills the house," I continued. "Their whispering turns to silence as the houselights dim. You, David, are ready to come out on the stage. You walk to the footlights, bow, and, as the enthusiastic applause dies down, you place your violin under your chin. And now, I want you to play for me just what you'll play for that audience."

David was transfixed. He boldly raised his instrument, positioned his bow—then paused and looked at me and said, "E?... or G?"

Man vs. Machine

WHILE sponsors and network programmers repeatedly urged us to "keep it funny," they also lobbied strongly for more *physical* humor on "Candid Camera." Many of our sequences, although funny, were light on the type of fast action that television seems to thrive upon. Fortunately, we discovered decades ago that we could be physical and funny whenever we pitted people against machines.

The simplest way to rig a machine is to disconnect the "off" switch. Thus, you have office workers bedeviled by a copying machine that wouldn't stop spewing copies; bakery employees trying to decorate cakes on a conveyor belt that wouldn't stop or slow down; customers in a self-serve ice cream parlor where the yogurt machine kept gushing; and secretaries using an electric sharpener that ground their pencils to bits.

Another favorite tactic is to invent new machines. This gave us the Auto-Medic, a coin-operated, do-it-yourself medical exam; the Beaut-o-matic, a sixty-second, mechanized beauty make-over; and the Eater-Meter, which allowed restaurant patrons to compute their check based upon the speed with which they ate their meal.

We've also enjoyed adding human features to otherwise ordinary machines. This gave us a "talking" photo machine ("surely you can smile better than that"); a hand in a washing machine that yanked the clothes back inside; and a telephone answering machine whose questions became increasingly specific.

131

Since people tend to take machines for granted, we found it fun to build an elevator that went sideways rather than up and down. We told taxi drivers to "follow that car," and sent them after an auto that split in two—with the halves heading in different directions. We put secretaries to work with a typewriter whose carriage flew off and landed in a wastebasket.

And there's always room on our show for a machine that does absolutely nothing. So we built one and offered it for sale in the appliance section of a department store. The very first shopper to come along said she wouldn't buy one...unless it came in a darker color.

All the World's a Stage

I had a rule when dealing with the network: if I wanted to do something, and I knew the answer would be no, I didn't ask for permission. I just went ahead and did it and dealt with the consequences later.

In this case I knew CBS's answer would be a resounding no. So, without a word, I rounded up my crew and boarded a jet. When we arrived and checked into a hotel, none of us spoke as we were shown to our room. Once we were alone, I signaled to our soundman to check the place out. He looked around and, hidden in the most obvious places, were nine microphones. It didn't surprise me. After all this was Moscow, and the year was 1961.

It was a time when the Cold War between the Soviet Union and the United States was at its coldest. In another year these two superpowers would go eye-to-eye in a nuclear showdown which would become known as the Cuban Missile Crisis.

The reason I hadn't asked CBS for permission to make this trip was that I was on a subversive mission—I wanted to show American audiences that the Soviets were actually human beings. I felt that my film clips would reveal that the average citizens were not the militant bears drawn by political cartoonists of the time. I wanted to show that the Russian people, in a land where my father was born, had amusing and identifiable foibles that Americans could relate to.

At that time virtually no passes were granted to members of the press to photograph inside Russia. However, we were able to obtain visas by posing as tourists. I had nightmares for a week or so before we left, and on the flight, my stomach was tied in knots. I knew the whole thing could fall apart as soon as we landed. All they needed to do was open our luggage. Our equipment didn't look suspicious—we took 16 mm cameras that amateurs often used—but how would I explain carrying 90,000 feet of film? Luckily, when we landed in Moscow, we got our first break—they waved us through customs without even opening our bags.

As we drove from the airport, I could feel tension building among the crew. Tension was always high when we shot "Candid Camera" scenes because of the unpredictability of human nature. But now we were playing for much higher stakes. For all we knew, the KGB might throw us in a Siberian prison camp, and we'd never be heard from again.

We had been assigned an "Intourist" guide who was supposed to accompany us for the entire trip, no doubt to keep us on the state-approved tour route. Despite her presence, I motioned for Mike Zingale and Pat Terzini, our cameramen, to surreptitiously begin shooting as we drove to our hotel. There was no gag. We just wanted to capture scenes of Moscow and Russian faces.

That clip showed how, unlike New York City, Moscow's streets contained few cars and trucks. Most people were on foot or rode bicycles. We had to drive slowly because people walked in the streets without watching for cars. In one case, we almost mowed down a man who had to jump aside to avoid our car.

The next day we did some filming from our hotel room window, and on the third day I began trying to give our Russian guide the slip. I took her on a shopping trip while Mike and Pat went off in another direction and spent the day filming. On the fourth day we took a gamble by changing hotels and leaving our guide behind. From then on we had more freedom to explore the city and photograph what we saw.

On that trip we used very few set-up gags; we simply wanted to capture slices of life in Moscow. The political division between our two countries was so great that most Americans were led to believe that there were daily military parades through Red Square with Communists waving rifles and chanting anti-American slogans. Instead, we photographed people working, shopping, talking on street corners, and peacefully going about ordinary lives.

While the similarities between our ways of life were apparent, there were some interesting differences. For example, we soon noticed many Russian women working in jobs that required heavy labor. That wouldn't seem as odd to us today. But back then, it was still unusual for American audiences to see women in this role. The Russians must have been reluctant to reveal this to visitors because they kept steering us away from places where women were doing construction work.

In one of the parks in Moscow, we shot a lengthy piece which was easily identifiable to Americans. The scene took place in front of a large cannon where Soviet tourists frequently posed for photographs. What we saw was the universal struggle of people who are trying to look good for posterity. This took several forms which were quite funny—and somewhat touching.

One man was determined not to have other tourists on the cannon behind his family. He would get himself, his wife, and children carefully arranged, prepare to have the picture taken, then glance over his shoulder. Sure enough, several people had wandered into the background. He'd shoo them away, then start the whole process again. It went on so long it became ridiculous—and ultimately he was unsuccessful.

What was most striking about this picture-taking sequence, though, was that it was apparently the accepted practice in Russia *not* to smile when a picture was being taken. It reminded me of the tintypes in America in the 1880s when photography was a very serious matter. The faces of these Russian families were absolutely stern. One man inspected his family carefully, making sure there wasn't a trace of a smile in their expressions. Just before the shutter snapped, a sixth sense told him something was wrong. He looked over and saw a smile shyly emerging on his wife's lips. As soon as he scowled at her, the smile disappeared, and the picture was taken.

"Candid Camera" had always been successful at capturing these small moments of daily life. But now I was in a foreign land—the homeland of our enemy—where I couldn't even rely on the spoken word to bridge the cultural gap (I had decided most of the clips would be silent; no dialogue or awkward sub-titles). I had to depend on pictures to show Americans the human side.

Before this trip, we had filmed in many countries, and in all fifty U.S. states. These travels, and the various gags we did in each location, showed that while regional differences existed, there were fundamental human responses to many situations.

One of the most interesting studies we did examined the quality of mercy. In a simple piece, inspired by the story of the

Good Samaritan, we had one of our "Candid Camera" performers lie in the gutter. We photographed the people passing by, to see who would stop to help. Then we changed the setup. For instance, we wanted to see what would happen if the man in the gutter was dressed in a tuxedo. We discovered that there was a certain snobbishness to people's feelings of mercy. If the man in the gutter was in a tux, they would pick him up in a minute; if he was dressed in rags, they'd let him lie there all day.

Another piece which we tried throughout the U.S. was called "Seven Free Things." We identified seven things you could probably get for free from a stranger: directions, a light for a cigarette, the time of day, change for a quarter, assistance holding a package, the loan of a pencil, and the use of a person's back to write on.

While this sequence disproved certain stereotypes, it actually proved others. We discovered that midwesterners were, as you might expect, fairly friendly. Californians followed no real pattern. To our surprise, we discovered that the people of Philadelphia, the City of Brotherly Love, were the least loving. On the other hand, people in the South really did provide southern hospitality—they would give you the seven free things, then invite you to dinner.

On our trip to Russia, we decided to try a piece we had done at home and abroad. A woman would stop a man on the street and say, "I've been carrying this suitcase all the way from the train station, and I'm worn out. Would you carry it the rest of the way for me?" Most men would quickly agree. What they didn't know was that the suitcase was filled with rocks! It weighed about two hundred pounds.

In New York every guy we asked would rather get a hernia than admit he couldn't lift the suitcase. But in London an interesting thing happened. When an Englishman couldn't get the suitcase off the ground, he stopped another man and together they were able to carry it away.

In France, we discovered that when Parisian men didn't want to do something, they pretended not to understand what we were asking them to do. It happened time after time. The woman asked men for help in perfect French, but they just shrugged their shoulders and kept walking.

When we went to Berlin, we improved the gag a bit. Instead of using rocks, we buried an iron plate in the ground and put a powerful electromagnet in the bag. Now the suitcase was impossible for our subject to lift, but with a flip of a switch in the bag's handle, our actress could easily carry it away. We also used this device in Italy—with unfortunate results. When we stopped a Roman with the standard request, he strained to lift the suitcase but couldn't get it off the ground. Our lady said to him, "That's all right, I'll do it myself," and walked off with it. This was apparently so damaging to his ego that the guy soon reappeared with about twenty relatives, ready to run us out of town.

Now it was time to try the suitcase gag in Moscow to see how the Russians handled it. We hired a Russian woman to make the request so there was no indication that we were foreigners. We didn't have the electromagnet, so we used sash weights from an elevator. It took two of our crew members to handle the suitcase.

The first thing we noticed was that we got more flat refusals than in any other city. This confused me because the Muscovites were generally rather friendly. Then something happened which explained the behavior. We asked one man for help, and the woman who was with him became very angry. Before we knew it, she had run off and come back with a policeman. I was sure she had spotted the hidden camera and was telling the cop that we were spies. But after a few minutes of arguing in heated Russian, our interpreter turned to me and said the woman was upset about something else—she was angry that this woman was asking for help. Apparently in Moscow there was no double standard. A woman carries her own bag—sash weights and all. The policeman listened but did nothing about it.

Later that day we filmed another memorable scene using the heavy suitcase. A gentleman came walking down the street wearing what looked to us like pajamas. (We later learned he was from one of the Soviet republics where this was their usual style of dress.) When our woman asked him for help, he picked up the two-hundred-pound suitcase like it was empty and walked away with it!

A year earlier we had done a popular piece in New York in which Tom O'Malley read other people's newspapers over their shoulders. We decided we would try this in the great Moscow subway. Again, we were nervous because filming as a tourist was one thing but using a hidden camera was much more risky. Mike Zingale concealed the camera in a cardboard box and pretended to fall asleep so he could look down into the viewfinder.

Although I couldn't read a word of Russian, I pretended to be interested in a newspaper article held by one of my fellow passengers. He gave me a strange look, which I responded to with a wave of my hand. He went back to reading, and so did I. Finally, I reached for the newspaper and steadily took possession of it. Now it was his turn to try to read over my shoulder—except I creased the paper so that he couldn't quite see it. If I had done that in Manhattan, I would probably have been punched in the nose.

As the end of our trip approached, and I became more convinced that we had all the elements of a strong show, I began to confront the question of how to get the film out of the country. I knew we couldn't count on passing freely through customs again. I became so concerned with finding a safe way to smuggle the film out that I even contacted Marvin Kalb who was then the CBS correspondent in Moscow. Unfortunately, he had no solution—and offered little hope. He said the regulations were arbitrarily enforced.

After fifteen days of shooting, we left for the airport and, for the second time, we were waved through customs. With a great sense of relief, we boarded the Soviet airliner and flew back to New York. I was anxious to get the film developed to see what we had, but when I screened the footage, my heart dropped. Much of the film was destroyed; the remainder was slightly fogged at ten second intervals. Apparently, the Russian officials, knowing full well of our activities, had attempted to destroy all the film, perhaps as it was passed through the baggage service.

I was devastated—but still determined to use the remaining footage to create a show. The film wasn't hard to watch; it was just not up to the usual broadcast standards required by network television. As we edited a rough cut, word leaked out about our trip, and the CBS programming people made it known that they wanted to see all the footage before it aired. I had expected this. The time had come to test my decision not to ask for permission first.

The screening room was filled with all the top programming executives. As the film began, what I noticed first, and what alarmed me, was the lack of any audible reaction. I knew this was a bad sign. They considered "Candid Camera" to be a comedy, and as such, they wanted laughs. Time and again they told me, "Keep it broad. Keep it funny. Don't get artistic." Here I had done something even worse then getting artistic—I had gotten political. As I sat in that dark, silent room, I knew I was in trouble.

When the show ended and the lights came back up, one of the vice presidents looked around at his cohorts. They seemed to shake their heads or indicate their disapproval in some way because he turned to me and said, "Allen, you've done a—well, *interesting* thing here. But it's obvious we can't air it."

I felt my anger building but kept the lid on. "Why?"

His answer surprised me. "The quality. I don't know what you did to the film. But it's not suitable for broadcast."

"The quality's good enough," I said. "Besides, this is too important to worry about quality."

He sighed deeply. "I'm sure you'll agree that the network needs to keep up certain standards of quality and —"

"Come on!" I said. "You think you're going to look like a bunch of Communists if you air this."

"Allen, don't be ridiculous. You've done a very noble thing here. But we just can't put it on TV. People would be adjusting their sets—our switchboard would go crazy..."

I knew they would protest the show. But it infuriated me that they pretended it was only the quality of the film they objected to.

I was close to saying something I would regret. But I was banking on the fact that, as the producer of one of the top shows on TV at that time, I had some clout too.

Instead of flying into a tirade, I simply said, "Okay, let's get Bill down here." That did the trick. Everyone stared at me.

"Allen, there's no need for that. He's just gonna say the same thing we already —"

I cut him off. "Get Mr. Paley down here. I want him to see this."

That was my ace—and one that I could play perhaps only once in my career. As head of CBS, Bill Paley was a figure who was shrouded in mystery. But he also had a reputation for being tough, strong and, most importantly, for thinking independently. I felt if I could just get him to watch the show, he'd be on my side.

A few days later I returned to the screening room and watched the footage with Bill Paley and the programmers. When the lights came up again, they started in on him immediately about the quality of the film, the lack of comedy, and the delicacy of political conditions. He waved his hand and cut them off.

"Let it go," he said. "I don't care about the quality. It's important."

The show was broadcast October 15, 1961.

In the next day's *New York Times* the television critic wrote: "Mr. Funt's random camera vignettes of people in Moscow were decidedly worthwhile. The series of pictures were warmly human." *Variety* went one step further: "Some seldom-seen views of the average Russians made Allen Funt's 'Candid Camera' via CBS-TV a memorable program."

It's always nice to be praised by the press. But the reaction that meant the most to me came in a letter to the editor of *TV Guide* from a woman in New Jersey: "I know that the program is aimed at laughs, but I believe it has accomplished more than that. After viewing the program I was left with a very strong feeling that the Russians are no different than we are. "

Candid Categories

L I K E any other business, "Candid Camera" depends on certain formulas for its success. Over the years, we've developed key categories from which our stunts are drawn.

REVERSAL: Creating situations where conventional or common expectations are reversed. For example, I once pleaded with a cop to write me a ticket for a parking violation I claimed to have been guilty of the day before. Another time, we drove into gas stations and asked the attendant to *remove* five gallons.

AUTHORITY: Using the power of authority to elicit compliance. We once got customers in an art gallery to keep changing their opinions about a painting as an alleged art expert changed his.

FAKING: Taking advantage of the fact that most people would rather fake it than admit to not knowing something, such as how to divide seven-eighths by three-quarters.

FANTASY: Playing out roles that viewers wish they could do themselves, for instance, talking back to a cop.

SIGNS: Showing the power of printed signs in our society. Our most successful was "Walk on White Squares Only" on a white-and-black linoleum floor. Another was changing the signs on rest room doors to "Us" and "Them."

PRIVACY: Showing how people act differently in private. For example, a teenage girl is perfectly composed when greeted by a handsome new teacher but falls apart as soon as he leaves the room.

THE BIZARRE: Placing a trained chimp, dressed in suit and tie, behind the counter in a dry cleaning shop and finding that people treat him, as they would any other shopkeeper. Sometimes it's funny if people don't acknowledge the bizarre, but it must be apparent that they've seen it and then pretend not to. Despite our best efforts, it doesn't always work.

Once we had a knight in full armor emerge from a sewer in New York City. Most people passed right by without any indication that they had noticed him.

The Cleanest "Dirty" Movie

The camera was hidden behind a folding screen at the end of the hallway. Our "subject"—a middle-aged man in a tan raincoat—had just stepped out of a nearby office and was waiting for the elevator. As far as he knew, it was a completely normal day. What he didn't know was that he was about to star in perhaps the cleanest dirty movie ever made.

With a discreet *ding* the elevator arrived, and the doors rumbled open. Our subject's slightly bored expression was immediately wiped off his face. He retreated half a step, and his jaw dropped as he stared through the open doors. A moment later, a pretty young woman stepped off the elevator wearing only high heels, a straw hat and a pleasant smile.

"Is Mr. Price's office on this floor?" she asked.

The man stammered out something to the effect that he wasn't sure, taking great care to keep his eyes from moving below her shoulder level. But then, as she turned and walked down the hall, he inspected every inch of her naked body.

Soon she returned and stood next to him, and together they waited for the elevator. You could feel the man's discomfort fill the hallway. He couldn't look at her—but he couldn't seem to make himself look away either.

Watching this title segment of my feature film, *What Do You Say to a Naked Lady?*, you would never guess that it was made in the late sixties at the height of the Sexual Revolution. Since the first love-ins at Haight-Ashbury, the young people in our country were supposedly tearing down the old standards of repression and hypocrisy. But we found that while the Sexual Revolution had changed many young people, countless older people still seemed to be living with almost-Victorian moral standards.

My desire to make a feature film had started several years earlier while "Candid Camera" was still on CBS. I knew the show wouldn't last forever, so I wanted to be ready for the next step. Sure enough, by 1968, after eight years on CBS, the show's ratings had slipped, and I received word that it would be canceled. No one likes to get canceled, but I was ready for a change.

When you work in television, your job is to offend no one. But in doing so, you wind up with a lot of mild and tightly controlled material. Eight years of doing network television had left me typecast and eager to make a statement.

There was, however, one big problem for me in making a feature film: I couldn't adhere to the discipline of shooting a traditional script. I once heard that French moviemakers have the luxury of not knowing today what they're going to shoot tomorrow. When I heard that, I thought, let me create one scene at a time, and I'll make a good movie.

There was another factor that kept me from shooting a film based on a screenplay. Years of making "Candid Camera" had proved how the unpredictability of real life, and the words and actions of real people, are much more gripping than the made-up dialogue of writers.

My intention was to find a topic that was significant enough to justify feature length, yet could be filmed using a hidden camera. I kicked around several themes and went to Hollywood to meet with studio execs. But everything I pitched was rejected. My days in advertising had shown me that if you want to sell something, it's best to include a sexual angle, so I decided to try to sell the studios on the idea of a film that humorously examined the attitudes of Americans toward nudity and sex.

My agent, Ted Ashley, set up a meeting with United Artists. Ted was the nephew of someone important at William Morris, and he had plenty of chutzpah. One of his more creative ideas was to collect commissions from his clients—*in advance.* He convinced me and several other clients that we should pay him our commissions up front, even when we weren't working. This plan allowed Ted to start his own agency—an agency that became big enough to buy Warner Brothers.

I've never been a great fan of agents. It seems to me that agents are only effective when something is already sold. Then the agent comes in and negotiates the terms and closes the deal. Still, there was a certain magic in the way Ted handled people, so I asked him to come along with me when I went to pitch my idea to David Picker at United Artists.

We arrived in Picker's office, and soon Picker and Ted were schmoozing about everything under the sun—except my movie. I assumed Ted would steer the subject back to my project, but an hour went by without his even mentioning it. Then, as we rose and were standing by the door, I gave Ted a look like, "What the hell's going on here?"

This must have jogged his memory because he turned to Picker and simply said, "Allen has a picture." Dramatic pause. "It's a good picture." Another pause. "It's 'Candid Camera' with sex."

Picker let this sink in. Then he asked, "What's the budget?"

"Five hundred thousand," Ted replied.

"Excuse me," Picker said, and abruptly disappeared.

When he was gone, I turned to Ted, totally confused. He acted as if this was all very normal.

"What in the name of God is going on here?" I asked.

Ted yawned. "David Picker can say yes to anything up to $400,000. If it's over that, he has to see Arthur Krim, the head of the studio."

Five minutes later, Picker came back and uttered one word, "Okay."

For the next two years, we traveled around the world shooting some of the funniest, most thought-provoking, and poignant scenes of my career. It was such a wonderful relief from the disciplines of doing a half-hour TV show.

(Incidentally, we soon discovered that the shooting ratio was much higher than what we were used to. On "Candid Camera" we had a 20-to-1 shooting ratio, meaning we photographed twenty people for every one we used. On *Naked Lady* the filming ratio was 200-to-1. Much of the budget was spent on raw film stock.)

Making *Naked Lady* was a chance for me to work out my own feelings on the subjects of nudity and sex. While I enjoy the sight of the female form, I am as hung up about sexuality as many of the people I captured on the film. I don't like risqué shows; I walked out of the sexy Broadway musical *Oh Calcutta!* So I was determined from the beginning not to make what people would think was a "dirty" movie.

I was also aware that, while I wanted to reverse the type-casting that had come from years of "Candid Camera," I didn't want the little old ladies in Des Moines to think that I had become a pervert.

As the title implied, many of the scenes in *Naked Lady* revolved around people's response to nudity which comes in many varieties and degrees. Our first challenge, then, was to decide how naked the "naked lady" should be. In the elevator scene, we tried dressing our actress in a G-string—but that looked much more lascivious than total nudity. But if the woman were totally nude, then the question became, where would we hide the microphone? The answer was, in her purse, of course.

As filming progressed, we were faced with another problem, because in many countries, including our own, it is illegal to appear naked in public. We wanted to do a scene where motorists were confronted by a naked hitchhiker, and we tried it in the most staid-seeming country, England. The British not only agreed to let us do the scene but loaned us several police officers to help with filming.

While many of these nude sequences were pure "Candid Camera" in style, designed mainly for laughs, other scenes delved deeper into social behavior. For example, a New England college class was told that it would be hearing a lecture on sex education by a guest speaker. Moments later a young, pretty—and completely naked—woman walked into the classroom and said, "Today we'll be talking about erogenous zones." The room was very quiet, and all eyes were on the lecturer. But there was no visible or audible reaction. They took it all in stride.

For purposes of comparison, we then found a similar class of middle-aged women and tried the same experiment. They completely fell apart. One woman collapsed in nervous laughter. Another woman walked out. Clearly there was a difference between these generations.

Another part of the film which drew a lot of attention was a series of hidden-camera interviews with teenagers talking about their sexual experiences. One young man claimed he'd been having intercourse since he was eleven. Another, still in his early teens, claimed he'd "scored" with eighty-three different women. A fifteen-year-old girl said she no longer found it necessary to "ball" every guy she met; she now had to *feel* something for him before she would have sex. But one young woman folded her arms across her chest and told us she just didn't want to discuss it. Furthermore, she had decided there was nothing wrong with being "virtuous." Her reaction was a refreshing change from the others, and we included her "non-revelation."

I must admit that while filming *Naked Lady* I felt nervous about what my children's reactions would be. I decided that the best approach was to be open. When we were done shooting, I screened the material for my kids and asked for their input.

Patty, who was about eighteen at the time, said, "Dad, you can't do this film without putting a naked man in it."

I told her that a nude woman can be confronted in real life without any great to-do. But seeing a nude man in public might cause more of an uproar than we could handle.

She wasn't convinced, "There has to be a way to show the other side of the subject. It's just not balanced as it is."

Her comments changed my thinking. There should be a man in it—and he should be nude. But I didn't know how to do this in an interesting way. Then I remembered that in art school we often used nude male models. Surprisingly, the women in our class had no reaction to male nudity beyond a professional interest; they were art objects and nothing more. But if the models moved or talked, the wall of silence was shattered, and the women focused on the fact that the models were human beings—and naked, at that.

For the movie we brought women to an art studio where a nude man sat in an artistic pose on a small riser, ready to be drawn or painted. The women we filmed showed a slight reaction when they first saw this man. On the whole, though, they soon relaxed and accepted him. But when he asked them for a cigarette, or tried to chat, they became increasingly uncomfortable. The scene really worked—but it caused a problem in another way, as I'll soon describe.

As we concluded filming, I began to feel that we had many strong, but isolated, scenes. What I lacked was a device to make a cohesive movie out of these separate scenes that would sustain an audience's interest for an hour and a half.

While wrestling with this problem, I was encouraged by the fact that the public's taste had recently strayed from the linear storytelling of the early days of moviemaking. Audiences were more sophisticated, more willing to experience film on a moment-to-moment basis without lengthy introductions.

I decided to rent a small screening room and invited a sampling of people to view the film—men and women, from teenagers to senior citizens—and told them that the movie would be stopped occasionally to get their comments. What we didn't tell them was that their discussion, which became quite lively at times, would be secretly filmed. In other words, we used a hidden camera to capture people's responses to hidden-camera scenes.

This screening audience expressed the very conflicts which I imagine general audiences felt after *Naked Lady* was released. While some were comfortable with the on-screen nudity and frank treatment of sex, others were dead against our film and told me so. This debate occurred many times, and we edited the most interesting highlights of the discussion into the movie, providing subtle transitions between some scenes, while avoiding the need for formal introductions.

With a rough cut completed, and an opening date approaching, I needed one more ingredient: a title. Somehow, a way to describe this unusual, eclectic movie eluded me. We kicked around hundreds of possibilities, but none seemed right.

One day I was screening the final cut with an editor. After it was over he asked, "What's the point of the movie?"

We all sat there in silence for a moment. Then I heard myself say, "What do you say to a naked lady?" Bingo. The title had popped out—and it stuck.

The period before the release of a movie is filled with many last-minute details—publicity, advertising, arrangements for opening night. My mind was on all these things. So the call I got from an executive at United Artists was a complete shock.

"Allen," he said. "Did you see the trades?"

I find that the less creative your job in the entertainment industry, the more you read the "trades"—the *Hollywood Reporter* and *Variety*. I just didn't have time to read who had been promoted to what position and what other film was about to be released.

"No," I answered. "I didn't see the trades." The connection with Hollywood crackled as I waited for him to continue.

"You got an X-rating."

I've always thought it was an interesting way to phrase it. "*I* got an X-rating."

He continued ominously, "You know what this means. We're going to have *major* problems marketing this thing."

As I hung up, I searched my mind for an explanation for this catastrophe. That same year a movie had been released in which a person was decapitated and the head was boiled in a pot of water. That movie got an R-rating. We didn't show scenes of anyone being hurt or mutilated; we merely featured people without clothes on. Why did we get an X?

It didn't take me long to figure it out. I could tell you, but I have found a more eloquent description in a review which someone sent me from the *Hollywood Reporter:* "Since it has virtually no perversion, less female nudity than many an R-rated film, a healthier attitude about sex than most GP-rated films and none of the dehumanizing violence of G-rated films, we may assume that 'Lady?' gets its rap for the exposed penis of an art class model in one of the sequences."

I've often thought that the two biggest hang-ups about sexuality are the way women worry about the size of their breasts and men worry about the size of their penis. Apparently this concern is age-old. Even as far back as the Greeks, there was an agreement among the sculptors to protect the egos of the males in the viewing public by portraying all men as being about the same size. I once tried to envision the meeting of all Greek sculptors in which this conspiracy was born. After a long discussion, they agreed to depict all men as "medium."

The same philosophy must have been in effect in the entertainment business in the Twentieth Century. The censors—a largely male group—were very open-minded about female nudity. But put a naked man in the movie, one who was a bit bigger than a "medium," and they brand it with an X-rating.

While I first thought the X-rating was the kiss of death, it turned out to be a blessing in disguise. At the same time, United Artists was releasing another X-rated film, *Last Tango in Paris.* They needed a second film to pair it with in theaters, but not a skin flick. Furthermore, *Midnight Cowboy,* which had been released the year before, was X-rated, and it did well at the box office. However, I didn't realize what the X-rating was worth at the time. Instead, I fumed about the double standard of the censors as I prepared for opening night.

Since I wasn't part of the Hollywood community, it was assumed I would hold the opening in New York City. But I can never do things in the normal way. It was such an offbeat movie, it needed an offbeat setting. Besides, I was beginning to sense that what I had made was fairly controversial. With this in mind, I decided to take it to a group of people who always embrace controversy: students. I planned an opening-night screening and party at my alma mater, Cornell University.

As a student there in the 1930s, I was a nobody. Now, on a snowy February night in 1970, I returned to Ithaca in triumph with a feature film to show the students—and a naughty one at that. I was nervous about their response to the movie, but I didn't have to wait long for their reaction. Right from the opening sequence, they tore the place apart. It was the one and only time I felt like a star. To get that kind of welcome from the students meant more to me than praise from the loftiest critic.

As the reviews came out, I found I did fairly well with the critics too. What I enjoyed most was the wide range of opinions and the passionate feelings which *Naked Lady* evoked. As a reviewer in the *Houston Post* wrote, "It's hilarious. It's heart-warming. It'll make a lot of people very mad."

One of the angriest reviews appeared in the now-defunct *Chicago Today*: "It is by far the cruelest thing Funt ever has done. He has put people in incredible situations and made fools of them about a very private subject—sex.

"He has made use of their ignorance and unsophistica-tion—or their sophistication to make money for himself. And I don't care if they DID sign releases—we all yearn for a little fame. It is the conscienceless way Funt has capitalized on this desire that is so annoying."

Another Chicagoan, Gene Siskel, had a different reaction: "I found *Naked Lady* to be a fresh look at stale attitudes. The film can be appreciated as both solid entertainment ... and as potent information."

A reviewer for *Motion Picture* picked up on the controversy and went so far as to attack fellow reviewers who disliked the film. "Critics who find *Naked Lady* exploitatively immoral and dishonestly intended are ignoring their function as artistic judges. They are allowing their own individual conservatism to interfere with an assessment of the film's value as bipartisan commentary."

Ultimately, Hollywood bases *its* judgment of a film's success on how much money it makes. By this definition *Naked Lady* was a big hit in its time. Costing only $570,000 to make, it grossed well over $5 million.

The financial success was secondary to the fact that I had fulfilled my own goal. I had taken the "Candid Camera" format and extended it to feature length. Moreover, I had used humor and entertainment to examine a subject which underlies much of our behavior.

The success of *Naked Lady* opened the door for another project which consumed much of my energy during the 1980s. Starting on HBO, and later moving to The Playboy Channel, I produced thirty-seven half-hour shows that poked fun at the way people react to nudity and sex. While these shows were not as thought-provoking as *Naked Lady*, they developed quite an audience and are still popular today on videocassette.

As *Naked Lady* continued its run, it created controversy wherever it went. A showing at a Newark, Delaware, drive-in was stopped because some nearby residents were afraid their children were watching on the sly. In Windsor, Connecticut, a citizen complained that the movie was "obscene," and a local judge ordered the theater where it was showing closed. The local sheriff went into the projection booth, watched the movie for about forty-five minutes, then stopped the film and arrested the theater owner. The print was seized, and the theater owner briefly jailed.

Another level of absurdity was reached when we were sued by a man who appeared in the film. Several people who had signed releases were surprised when the movie came out to find themselves in an X-rated film. Our insurance company settled some of the claims, but one was so ridiculous we promptly went to court.

The plaintiff was Ray Tillman, an eighty-six-year-old man who had been filmed with three other residents of a senior citizens' home in Montclair, New Jersey. They had been asked to give their opinions about a statue the facility was about to receive as a gift. It was a copy of Michelangelo's David, and the question put to the senior citizens was whether David should be presented naked or attired in a fig leaf.

The argument was prolonged and passionate. Tillman argued strongly that the statue would offend the dignity of the elderly and threaten the morals of the young unless it was fig-leafed. But an eighty-five-year-old woman with him countered, "If you put a fig leaf on, the kids will just lift it up." The argument was still raging when I appeared and told them all they were going to be in a movie. They good-naturedly signed releases. However, when the picture came out, Mr. Tillman claimed his friends had ridiculed him because he was in a movie featuring topless women.

Once in court, the plaintiff admitted he hadn't seen the movie and couldn't identify the people who were harassing him. He was awarded $4,000 for loss of dignity.

Mr. Tillman's case is another example of how our society distorts sex by treating it as taboo. It's rarely discussed openly and honestly. Instead, the subject is either shrouded in mystery or presented along with sneers and snickers. In a literal sense, we go to great lengths to hide (clothe) that which we call obscene. But it's the act of covering up which creates the obscenity. As I mentioned earlier, we discovered that a woman in a G-string is much nakeder than a woman who is fully nude. If people are allowed to peek now and then, but not see everything, the voyeuristic nature is inflamed.

I heard a story once about a man who noticed that the couple across the courtyard from his apartment had forgotten to pull their shades before making love. He turned off the light in his room and watched them. The next time this happened, he did the same thing—turned off his lights and watched them making love. This went on for weeks until, one night, the man forgot to turn out *his* light. Soon, the couple looked over and saw him watching them. They smiled, waved, and went back to making love. As soon as they did this, the man lost interest and went off to do other things.

No Release

MOST of the people caught on "Candid Camera" are only too eager to sign a release, which for nearly five decades has read as follows:

> I acknowledge that you have photographed me without my prior knowledge and without any preparation, coaching, or rehearsal. If this film is used, I will receive the sum of $50, in exchange for my irrevocable consent to use the silent and/or sound motion pictures in any way you see fit in perpetuity throughout the world, including use on television. I also agree that you may edit such motion pictures in any way you think proper without obtaining any further consent from me or making any additional payment to me.

Most people are so happy to learn that they've been on our show that I imagine they would sign almost anything, so in 99 percent of our work, getting a signed release is completely routine. The one-in-a-hundred subject who balks is usually someone we have caught in the wrong place, at the wrong time, with the wrong person.

Without question, the hardest place for us to get releases is a local movie theater on a weekday afternoon. Everybody in the theater, it seems, is supposed to be someplace else: salesmen goofing off, kids playing hooky, housewives with unfinished laundry at home.

We have also learned that certain restaurants, especially those in so-called "bedroom communities," present problems.

159

I recall one sequence, filmed on a Friday evening in Darien, Connecticut, in which we tried to get the reaction of couples when the waiter presented gifts "from an admirer" to the woman at the table. That night, our crew photographed eight different couples. We waited patiently after each take for all customers in the section to leave and new patrons to be seated. Six of the eight refused to sign releases; the men were with someone else's wife, or the women were with someone else's husband.

Sometimes, though, there is no predicting when efforts to get a release will fail. Once I tried a gag at a lunch counter in which the waitress intentionally poured so much coffee in the customer's cup that there was no room for cream or sugar. I sat at the counter egging on each customer to demand a fresh cup. One gentleman was unflappable—until I stepped away from the counter. All of a sudden, he turned beet red, raised his voice, and told the waitress, "That guy is a nut! You can take my word for it. I'm a psychiatrist."

His reaction, although heated, seemed rather innocent at the time. It never occurred to us as we approached the man for a release that a psychiatrist would not want to be exposed on national television as diagnosing a stranger as a nut after only a few minutes of conversation. "If anybody ever sees this film, it'll be the last picture you ever take!" he exploded. In an attempt to placate the doctor, we actually handed him the exposed film on the spot.

The next day, he called my office to ask if there were any copies in existence. The following day, he called for assurance that we had destroyed the negative (there was none). And a week later, the doctor's wife called to report that he was a nervous wreck, concerned that his career could be ruined.

Needless to say, we try to learn from our mistakes. Since that day, when asking the subject's name for a release, we always begin with, "Is it Mr., Mrs., or Dr.?"

White Gates, our 110-acre estate in Croton-on-Hudson, NY, (clockwise from bottom left) Evelyn and me; with John, Patricia and Peter; and my favorite English saddle horse, Gal.

Debbie, who won me over as Cinderella, at the Tic Toc Day School in Queens, NY.

George Gobel plays a sleepwalking patron at an all-night diner, in a piece we needed the next morning.

The toughest stunt ever: an upside down room in Seattle, with Peter supported only by a lap belt and a firm grip on his inverted chair.

Bess Myerson, my co-host in 1966, made it a very rewarding year.

William Saroyan, who created playlets with which we could contrast the drama of real life.

Durwood Kirby, co-host from 1961–1966, joins me in a sequence with guest Zsa Zsa Gabor.

Britain, even a bicyclist stopped to study our nude hitchhiker, in a scene from *What Do You Say to a Naked Lady?*

or the film "Money Talks," our stuntman enjoys a salad of dollar bills, while a mesmerized ustomer tries to digest the scene.

We've had many big-name
guests on "Candid Camera,"
including the lovable Lassie.

Marilyn, William and Juliet, in our duplex at the Beresford in Manhattan.

Directing my son Peter in intros, shot at my Hollywood house in Nichols Canyon.

Loni Anderson was a vivacious guest host for our 35th anniversary special in 1983.

Lynn Redgrave
joined me for our CBS
Christmas Special
in 1987.

Celebrating my 78th birthday at a villa in Florence are (standing, from left) William; Patricia, her daughter Katie and husband Ken; John; Juliet; Peter and wife Amy; (seated) Anne Flynn and my granddaughter Stephanie.

Money Talks

U nited Artists was so elated over the profits from *What Do You Say to a Naked Lady?* that I assumed I could easily strike a deal for my second feature film. I envisioned a hidden-camera treatment of society's second greatest hang-up after sex—money. However, UA wanted no part of the project.

It seems that when you make a fortune on your first picture, the deep thinkers in Hollywood assume you could never do it twice, and they won't back you. Several studios refused to even consider a second hidden-camera movie until I agreed to put up a big chunk of my own money. Once I did that, UA was willing to talk, and we soon signed a deal. Naturally, I called the film, *Money Talks.*

With the money in place, we went back on the road for eighteen months. At one stop, we summoned furriers to a posh hotel suite to fit a coat for a wealthy client, who turned out to be a huge Great Dane. We had an actress walk down a busy street dropping money, seemingly by accident, to see who would return it and who would pocket the bills. We cast Muhammad Ali as the recipient of a package, who tried to persuade the delivery boy to accept boxing lessons as payment instead of cash. We even hired a stuntman to sit at a lunch counter and casually eat a salad of dollar bills as startled customers looked on.

One of the best sequences in *Money Talks* took place in a bank, where we made the chain holding the ballpoint pen so short it was virtually impossible to write with. Unfortunately, our most exciting footage was never used in the movie.

In one take, a man was particularly funny to watch as he struggled to use the pen. Later, as we were getting his release, another fellow came over and asked, "Was I in the shot?" I told him he was. In response, he pulled out a gun and yelled, "Up against the wall!"

When the first man saw this, he assumed it was another element in the stunt and began laughing hysterically. The gunman screamed, "Shuddup," and the first guy laughed even louder. At this point I began laughing, and soon everyone in the bank was doubled over.

The gunman was frozen in frustration. He couldn't shoot, he couldn't speak, he couldn't even move. So the police walked in and made an easy arrest. The problem? We couldn't use the film without a release from the holdup man—and he wouldn't sign.

Maybe it was a bad omen that the funniest scene we shot never appeared in the movie. Despite some good reviews, including a near-rave in *Variety*, *Money Talks* was a box-office flop. It was yanked from theaters without even earning back its budget.

As was often the case on "Candid Camera," staffers from my office played small parts in the movie. One such role went to my friend and longtime accountant, George Samuals. After filming George's part, I offered him $1,000 for his appearance. In typically gracious style, he turned down the money.

As a professional people-watcher, I had been fascinated by George for many years. He had a funny way of misusing words—à la malapropist Norm Crosby—so he often called me his *mender*. I assumed he meant I was his *mentor*, but I always let it go. He also had a skin condition that was anything but humorous; it left him constantly scratching at himself, in obvious discomfort.

Over the years I learned much about George's family life, including the fact that his daughter was born with a rare birth defect that limited her learning ability.

George had joined my staff as a bookkeeper, and after nine years of reliable work, I hired him as our accountant. He had other show-business accounts where he reviewed records to make sure producers got a straight count from distributors. For example, if MGM was giving a producer a percentage for distributing his film, the producer might hire George to examine the books.

George was known to everyone on the staff to be a sweet and generous guy. Once, when Marilyn and I were away on a vacation, and one of our kids developed a high fever, it was George we called to handle the crisis. After the skyjacking to Cuba, George met us at the airport in New York to help us forget our trauma by inviting us to his son's bar mitzvah.

I'll never forget what an incredibly lavish affair the bar mitzvah turned out to be. It was held in a huge hall in the affluent Five Towns area of Long Island. George's wife greeted guests in a designer gown and changed several times during the evening into other custom-made dresses. The orchestra was the best in the area, and later it was replaced by a different dance band. Clearly, George had spared no expense—and he wanted everyone to know it.

"George," I said to him at one point, "you must have dropped a bundle on this thing. How can you afford it?"

"Life's been good to me," he replied. "This is an important day in my life. I want to share my blessings with my friends. And you're my very best friend, Allen."

Then he got choked up, as he sometimes did, scratched at his arm a few times, and hugged me. The embrace lasted a little longer than I thought the moment called for, but that was George.

If imitation is the sincerest form of flattery, I should have been quite flattered by George's behavior. He found out where I bought my suits and had his tailored there. We drove the same kind of car. He even ate at the same restaurants. But he did all this in such a complimentary way that I never thought there was anything strange about it.

While I was noticing how George imitated me, the rest of the staff noticed other things. George often traveled overseas with his wife and little girl; he dressed expensively; and he had an eye for flashy jewelry. He boasted to the staff that the bar mitzvah I'd attended had cost him more than $60,000.

But at the time, in 1972, I had too much on my mind to worry about George. This was a transitional time in my life. "Candid Camera" had finished its CBS run a few years earlier, and the excitement of *Naked Lady* had died down. My marriage to Marilyn, which began as such a passionate affair, had been reduced to a state of almost constant arguing. I was starting over again as a father too. Juliet and William were young, and I couldn't help worrying what the tension between Marilyn and me would do to them.

It was against this background that I discovered the truth about George. Before I explain, I have to add that the real name of my accountant was not George Samuals. His real name can be found in newspaper accounts of what happened. But I won't identify him here for his family's sake.

One day, a cameraman on my staff came into my office carrying a newspaper. He plunked it down on my desk and pointed to an article. "You better read this, Allen," he said.

The story was about an orchestra leader whose accountant misappropriated some of his money.

I finished reading and looked up. "Why are you showing me this?"

He said, "Well, you know, we all wonder about George."

I think I might have actually laughed at him. "Oh come on," I said. "George is a good friend. He'd never do anything like this."

"What about his car and his suits and the way he jets around the world—"

"Trust me. George has been with me for years and hasn't taken a dime that didn't belong to him."

"Okay," the cameraman said, standing up. "If you say so..."

He left me alone in my office with the newspaper still lying on my desk.

And the doubt began to set in.

It was late in the afternoon, but the banks were still open, so I called the Chemical Bank of New York. I knew we had an account there and, according to my records, there was a balance of more than $500,000. I identified myself to the clerk and asked for the current balance for Allen Funt Productions. Moments later the clerk came back with the answer, "$25,000."

I'll never forget the sinking feeling I had as I heard that. Nearly half a million dollars was gone!

I kept thinking there had to be a reasonable explanation. When I thought of George, I pictured his warm smile, his wife and little girl, his son's bar mitzvah where I was treated like the guest of honor. He just wouldn't do this to me.

George was working late that day so I called him into my office, hoping this could be explained in a matter of minutes. He came in with his usual greeting and smile, wearing a suit I recognized as similar to one I recently wore. I asked him to close the door, and I could tell he was tensing up. He sat down across from me, scratching a bit more than usual at his hands and neck.

"George, I just called Chemical Bank," I began. "We're supposed to have half a million bucks in there. They said we have twenty-five thousand. Now what the hell's this all about?"

I could see him redden. Quickly, maybe too quickly, he said, "Allen, I should have told you. I got a lead on a new stock that's gonna take off. I bought a couple thousand shares, and I figured I'd have the money back in the account before you noticed it."

"For Christ's sake, George. I've never once in my life played the stock market. You know that. You know everything about my money."

"This was a solid lead," he said. "I would have been stupid not to jump on it. But if it bothers you that much, I'll cash out."

He stood up and headed for the door. "Don't worry, Allen. Just leave it to me."

I wanted to believe him. I really did. But, before he reached the door I asked, "What's the name of your broker?"

He gave me a name and number and left. As soon as the door closed, I grabbed the phone. When the broker heard my voice, I felt him wither at the other end of the line. He asked if he could come over and see me immediately. He arrived about an hour later, looking terrified.

"I want you to know that I didn't take any of your money," he began. "Not a cent."

I held up my hand. "Look, I'm not accusing you of anything. I'm just trying to find out what the hell George is up to."

The broker licked his lips and spoke slowly, "George told me he was doing some things—with your money."

"Like what?"

"He—he didn't say. Moving it around or something, I think. He begged me to cover for him. But honest to God, I didn't touch a cent."

He had said enough. I began checking all my accounts, and I found discrepancies everywhere. When the losses were totaled, it turned out that he had taken about $3 million of my money—and borrowed another $250,000 in my name. The money George had taken was everything I had in the bank after twenty-four years of producing "Candid Camera." It was the money I needed to continue my work. It was my life's savings. And it was all gone.

In the weeks following the initial discovery, investigators questioned George and his family. Slowly, the primary motive for his embezzlement began to emerge. It turned out that his daughter's birth defect was hereditary, and the disease was traced to George's side of the family. Whether it was his own guilt, or his wife's accusations prodding him, George began siphoning large amounts of my money to pay for trips to see specialists all over the world.

George's main scheme worked this way: In the office we were always sending people out to buy things. I never knew what these purchases would cost so I'd give them a signed blank check. If they came back without buying anything, they returned the signed check to George. Over a period of years George collected thirty such blank checks. He then wrote checks to an account he controlled.

George also took several hundred thousand dollars from "petty cash"; he paid himself for services never rendered and regularly collected $6,000 himself every time he paid the weekly payroll of $6,000 for a staff of forty. He had my power of attorney and was thus able to negotiate the $250,000 loan in my name.

But investigators revealed one fact which haunted me more than any other. On the same day that George turned down $1,000 for his appearance in *Money Talks*, he had used my money to write himself a check for $50,000.

After years of high living, George's wife had apparently become suspicious about the source of their prosperity. He told her that I had made him a partner in the show. This lie soon backfired because as the show grew in popularity, and *Naked Lady* became a box-office hit, George's wife demanded that he ask me for a larger share of the profits. And so the amounts George had to embezzle increased.

One day during the investigation, the district attorney said he wanted to talk to me in his office. When I entered, I sensed tension in the room. He let me sit there in silence for a moment, his eyes on me the whole time.

"Mr. Funt," he finally said, "is there anything about this case you haven't told us?"

"You've taken my statement," I said. "I can't really think of anything to add."

"I'm talking now about something *besides* the statement," the DA said.

"What are you getting at?" I asked.

He didn't answer right away, but now it was obvious he was digging.

After another accusatory pause, he said, "Isn't it true that you made a great deal of money on that show of yours?"

"I told you that the first time. But I don't see —"

"And isn't it true that taxes took a big bite out of your profit?"

"Of course. But that's just part of doing business."

"But isn't it also true that if you could find a way to pay lower taxes, you could pocket a lot more money?"

I was so angry, I couldn't speak. Finally I controlled myself. "I'm out three million bucks, and *I'm* being treated like a crook. Why don't you just tell me what the hell you think I've done?"

This slowed him down, but he bounced back. "Mr. Funt, don't you think it's a little strange that Mr. Samuals, whom you accuse of embezzling your money, *paid taxes* on the money he supposedly took from you?"

This was as unexpected as a scene on "Candid Camera." It turned out that while stealing more than three million dollars, George retained some small shred of integrity and paid taxes on every dime he stole.

The DA apparently had no evidence of the scheme he was accusing me of—that is, siphoning money to someone who would pay taxes at a lower rate. So he quickly dropped this line of questioning and concentrated on the case against George. A short time later, forty-four counts of grand larceny were filed against George totaling $1,285,826, and covering a four-year period. (Although I'd actually lost about $3 million, this was the amount prosecutors felt they could prove he had embezzled.)

Since that first day in my office, when the embezzlement was discovered, I hadn't seen George face to face. I heard through various sources, however, that he was falling apart. His arraignment was postponed so his wife could commit him to a sanitarium on Long Island. George eventually pleaded guilty to all charges.

A short time later, the telephone rang in the middle of the night. It was the police informing me that George had checked into a Manhattan hotel and taken an overdose of pills. He was dead.

George's wife was, interestingly enough, able to collect $1 million from his life insurance policy. I sued for this money on the grounds that much of what George stole from me had been transferred to his wife's name. The court decided I was entitled to part of the insurance money, but most of that was consumed by legal fees.

I was broke. I had bills to pay. And my marriage was falling apart.

So far, it probably seems there is nothing at all funny about this story. But I've always felt there is a humorous side to everything that happens in life. Most of the time we're so wrapped up in our pain and self-pity that we don't see it. But once I find this humorous aspect, and I'm able to laugh, the blow is softened.

As I began to try to recover my money from other sources, I learned that George had made large contributions to his temple on Long Island. After his suicide, I allowed an appropriate length of time to pass and went to see the temple's leaders. While I was waiting to meet with them, I noticed there were plaques all over the walls commemorating George's acts of generosity. Finally, I was ushered in to meet with four gracious gentlemen, and I requested the return of the money George had given them. They said they would take the matter under consideration and get back to me.

A few days later, they telephoned with their decision. "We can't give you back any of the money," they said. "But we can change the name on the plaques to your name."

I hung up the phone, ready for another burst of anger. Instead, the full irony of the situation began to dawn on me. The more I thought about it, the funnier it became. After making all that money by tricking people on TV, I had become the victim of the biggest deception of all. Here was a man who took more money than most bank robbers. He took it with a smile and was exceedingly generous. Indeed, he paved a highway of goodwill—with my money. Everybody still loved George; worse, some people implied that my legal actions were responsible for his suicide.

Once I focused on the absurdities of the situation, I couldn't feel much anger for George. Pity, maybe, but not anger. Though I had no money in the bank, I was alive and had five wonderful children counting on me.

It was then that I realized I had to sell my beloved Alma-Tadema collection. So many things were coming to an end, it seemed that this love affair would have to end too. As I mentioned earlier, the Parke Bernet gallery offered to auction the paintings for a percentage or give me a guaranteed price. I went for the guaranteed price. The popularity of Alma-Tadema's paintings had grown enormously, and the auction prices were so high that it turned out I would have done better with a straight percentage. Still, proceeds from the sale kept me afloat.

Although I steadily rebuilt my finances after the embezzlement, it didn't help my relationship with Marilyn. With or without the money, we couldn't seem to find any peace in our marriage.

I used my marital dilemma as the basis for my third feature-length film, *Smile When You Say I Do*, which was produced for ABC-TV in 1973 as a "Movie of the Week." My favorite
scene involved a nursery school class in Florida that acted out a
wedding ceremony before our hidden cameras. The tot playing
the minister turned to the lad playing the groom and asked,
"Do you take this woman to be your awful wedded wife?"

As Marilyn and I began divorce proceedings, I was left with
time and money and the need for a change. There was nothing
left for me in New York. I began driving west and didn't stop
until I came to the other ocean.

A Form for Every Format

W E recently produced two "Candid Camera" videocassettes for business-training purposes, depicting potential problems in customer service. Our video distributor has a contract in which we grant the right "...to translate, sell, rent, lease, distribute, display, exhibit, license and otherwise market the program and any and all elements thereof, in all non-broadcast formats and configurations, in any language and in any and all media and/or markets throughout the world including, without limitation, by means of any and all forms of video devices of any kind or nature whatsoever including, without limitation, videocassettes and videodiscs in all formats and configurations, whether now existing or hereinafter developed."

I assume our distributor's lawyer was being paid by the word. But I'm most fascinated by the phrase, "whether existing or hereinafter developed"; it underscores the frantic pace at which the media are changing.

My own vision, back when "Candid Microphone" was launched in 1947, never included such things as videocassettes and videodiscs—we hardly knew anything about television. Yet, my single idea has not only endured, it has been successfully adapted for virtually every program format to come along.

After making the leap from radio to television, we also produced some forty "Candid Camera" shorts for Columbia Pictures. These were shown in theaters as an extra attraction with the feature film. Then came a half-dozen albums for Columbia Records, "A collection of off-guard conversation secretly recorded with hidden microphones; the actual, unrehearsed voices of everyday people caught in the act of being themselves."

By the late fifties, we branched out into what were known as "industrial films," for such firms as Shell Oil and Minneapolis Honeywell. Using hidden cameras, we illustrated various problems salespeople might encounter with new products or promotions.

The fifties also marked the publication of my first book based on "Candid Camera": *Eavesdropper at Large*. In it I wrote that, "I've often dreamed of making a full-length feature picture done entirely with hidden cameras." Of course, I've since done three of them—two for theaters and one for TV.

In the sixties I published my second book, *Candid Kids*, in which I recounted the charming comments of youngsters photographed for our show. By the eighties, "Candid Kids" became the name of an hourlong children's collection on videocassette. We also produced several "Best Of" cassettes with general "Candid Camera" content. And when our adult versions became popular on cable TV, they, too, were marketed worldwide on cassette.

Along the way, we've done hidden-camera commercials; developed a college psychology program; we even marketed a "Candid Camera" board game.

And we stand ready to put "Candid Camera" to work in other media, whether now existing or hereinafter developed.

Moving West

As we headed south on Pacific Coast Highway, the real estate agent droned on and on about the property we were going to see. I tuned him out. I was tired of looking for a new place to live, and I didn't even know why I'd agreed to come along with him. I'd already chosen an area I thought suited me, 50 miles to the north, in Santa Cruz. The problem was, I just couldn't find the right piece of property.

It was 1975, and for about a year now I had been drifting—physically and emotionally. "Candid Camera" was doing well in syndication. But the challenge of doing the show didn't consume me as it once had. As I entered my sixties, I found I was in search of not only a new home, but a new adventure as well.

I had spent the previous summer in Aspen, Colorado, and made several car trips through the West, looking for a place to buy. I soon narrowed my search to California, although I knew for sure I wanted no part of Los Angeles. L.A. is a city where everyone looks and acts like a movie extra. They dress in costumes, speak in no particular accent, and seem to be starring in a movie that is running in their heads. Beverly Hills is even worse. Everyone is in the entertainment business, and they are all competing to see who is the richest and most powerful person. Nothing suits me less.

Although I was a native of Brooklyn, I felt no pull to return to New York. The city had lost whatever appeal it once held for me. Instead, I had an urge to find the real West.

The agent hit the brakes as we approached a narrow bridge in the region called Big Sur. I looked over the railing, and far below my eye found the Pacific angrily pounding against boulders at the mouth of a small river. Farther out, dark strands of kelp swayed under the ocean's surface, and I thought I saw a sea lion twisting through the water.

"The property starts here and runs for a mile and a tenth south," the agent said. "The total parcel is 1,210 acres which is about two square miles."

I sat up a little straighter in my seat and looked in the direction he was pointing. All I could see were mountains, cliffs, and the bluest ocean I'd ever seen stretching to the horizon. *Two square miles*...I liked the sound of that.

"Now I warned you that the property's in pretty rough shape..." the agent said, signaling for a left turn, even though there wasn't a car in sight.

"Sure, sure," I said. "That doesn't bother me."

We turned and the car bumped onto a dirt road. We passed through a tall wooden gate, the kind you see on western ranches, and started climbing. The road cut back to the north and continued up to a high cliff.

"The owners have had this place for years," the agent explained. "It's kind of a strange situation. Two brothers who are married to two sisters. But they're all in their eighties so they can't take care of the property anymore."

I looked back over the edge of the cliff and down to the ocean. Two enormous rocks jutted out of the water, and the waves foamed around them. The sky was filled with scraps of clouds, and the sun shone brightly.

The agent steered carefully around a corner. And then I saw it—the most magical valley I'd ever laid eyes on.

The road gently descended between two broad mountains toward a weathered barn and several outbuildings. Then the road climbed again through pastures and groves of pine and cypress until it disappeared out of sight in the distance. Cattle grazed here and there. A colt frisked in a wood-railed corral.

The agent slowed to let a fox cross in front of us, then pulled up beside a ramshackle barn. He cut the engine and I stepped out. For a moment I savored the silence, thinking of the years I'd been assaulted by New York's constant din. But the valley was actually filled with sounds: the wind moaned in the trees, distant cattle called to each other, a hawk shrieked far above. Then I heard another sound.

"Too bad," I said. "You can hear the traffic on the road down there."

The agent gave me a strange look. "That's not traffic."

I listened again and realized he was right. It was a rhythmic sound, strong and insistent. It was the surf. Here we were a mile from the shore, high in the mountains, and the sound of the surf was so strong, I expected to look down and find sand under my feet. I knew then that I had to own this place. But an entire year passed before it was mine.

The brothers who owned the ranch knew what they wanted, and they wouldn't take a penny less. Although they were well into their eighties, they were convinced they could wait me out. I finally gave up and paid their asking price—something I've rarely done.

When I did get possession of the property, I rode and walked over every acre of the land and took stock of what I had. While the scenic beauty of the area was breathtaking, the property was in terrible shape. The land was eroded, the buildings were uninhabitable, drinking water was in short supply, and the roads were rutted and impassable for anything except a 4-wheel drive vehicle.

Still, while the actual condition of the property was poor, what I saw in my mind's eye was magnificent. I imagined a new barn big enough for dozens of horses; a ranch house with a large porch; hillsides and high pastures filled with cattle and horses.

In my various explorations of the property, I also discovered a cluster of old shacks about 700 feet up from the barn on the side of a mountain. From this site, I could look back down the valley and all the way to the Pacific, which appeared through two notches on either side of a knob of land. I began to think this might be a good location for another house—a guesthouse maybe. Slowly, the idea of creating what I later called the "Indian House" took shape in my mind. It would be rustic, but filled with Native American art.

During this time, we were taping the syndicated "Candid Camera" in Nashville. Still, every chance I got, I flew back to work on my ranch, living in an Airstream trailer near the old barn. And every time I arrived, I felt like a kid. I went to bed early and was up at dawn, working and planning, tinkering with a dozen projects or riding my horse to check on our cattle.

It soon became obvious that I needed someone to help me realize all the dreams I had for my ranch. I needed someone who knew horses and cattle, but could also dig wells, build

houses, fix farm machinery, mend fences, and—most importantly—someone who would love the place as much as I did.

Through the years, I've been lucky to find some very special
people to work with. It was true on "Candid Camera" and in my
private life too. In Croton, we had Rocky Caputo who helped
me renovate buildings, landscape the property, and dream up
and create various odd structures. After a few years on the
ranch, I met John Moon—and he's still working for me today,
sixteen years later.

John was in his early twenties when I hired him, and he
always reminded me of the Marlboro man. He dressed in
denim and was slow to answer any question. But when he did
speak, his words held a kind of cowboy wisdom. He was a salt-
of-the-earth, honest guy, and he knew how to do just about
everything. He was soon involved in helping me turn the place
into a working ranch.

Right away we ran smack into a major roadblock. When I
applied for building permits, I was told that everything hinged
on approval by the California Coastal Commission. Its mandate
is, of course, to preserve the beauty of the coastline. The way it
does this is to keep many things from being built.

I approached the commission with the naive idea that it
would recognize the beauty of my plans and quickly approve
them. Instead, the commissioners wanted me to agree never to
subdivide the property and to designate 500 acres as an histor-
ical site. In response to my proposal for the Indian House, to be
built high on the side of the mountain, they required me to
send up helium-filled balloons that would be at the exact
height of the finished structure. Since the balloons were visible
to a commissioner, in a car a mile away, I was told I couldn't
build the house.

For the next three years, I spent a fortune in legal fees wrestling with the Coastal Commission—and getting nothing done. To make matters worse, the first year I owned the property, the region was hit by a serious drought. The next year, we had the heaviest rain in decades. Sometimes the main road was washed out, and I had to take a county road high into the mountains, then cut back to my property. I spent hours pounding over dirt roads in the Jeep.

I found myself in a strange position. I had 1,210 acres of the most beautiful land in California, but the only place I could live was in a Airstream trailer. It seemed I might be waiting for the Coastal Commission to approve my plans for another three years.

When a house went up for sale adjacent to my ranch, I decided to buy it. The spacious house is situated beside the historic Bixby Bridge on top of a huge ocean-side cliff and is perhaps the most beautiful of the many wonderful houses I've owned.

I spent hundreds of hours expanding and furnishing the Bixby House, as I call it, but I got tired of driving fifteen miles into Carmel when I wanted a loaf of bread. After a short search, I bought a furnished house in Pebble Beach, never intending to stay there for long. I just wanted a place to hang my hat. Now, seventeen years later, I still own all three properties.

Although the renovation of the Bixby House was finished, and I was now living in Pebble Beach, I still yearned to complete my plans for the ranch. My lawyers, meanwhile, had been pushing our proposal to the Coastal Commission, but with no luck.

A short time later, I happened to go to a party a friend of mine threw in Carmel. I had been telling him about the problems I had getting building permits, so when I arrived he took me aside.

"There's someone here you really should meet," he said, pointing across the room. "That guy over there is the head of the Coastal Commission."

As I looked at this man, my anger rose. To me, he represented everything that was wrong with government. I had the urge to walk over there and chew him out—just to vent my frustrations. But I controlled myself and kept my mind focused on the vision I had for the ranch.

"You mind introducing me?" I asked. My friend led me across the room, and we shook hands. If my name meant anything to him other than "Candid Camera," he didn't show it.

I'm not a tactful person; I'm more apt to speak my mind and let the chips fall where they may. But I knew that what I was about to say could determine the future of my ranch, so I didn't jump down the guy's throat. Instead, I acknowledged the importance of the commission and praised its work. Then I slowly began to talk about how much I wanted my ranch to reflect the natural beauty of the coastline. I described my plans for the Indian House and spoke about the art I'd collected that captured the history and beauty of the area. I told him I was planning to build a barn on the site where one had been for more than a hundred years. I assured him that the roads would follow the same course they had always taken. I let my enthusiasm show and hoped it would become infectious.

A week later my lawyer called. The Coastal Commission had approved all our permits for the ranch.

John and I went to work immediately. We set up a sawmill on the property and began cutting and stockpiling redwood beams and planks for the barn and ranch house. I had designed a barn that would blend a classic New England feel with the rugged look of western buildings. It had room for fourteen horses and could store enough hay to feed the cattle all winter. It even had a complete shop where we could do everything from making furniture to rebuilding a truck engine. The centerpiece of the barn was an octagonal room surrounded by horse stalls. On the second story were balconies, and higher up, at the peak of the roof, were windows through which the mountaintops were visible. We used this area for showing horses, square dances, and even as the site of my daughter Patricia's wedding to Kenneth Oxman.

The ranch house was finished in a similar style, and then we set to work building and decorating the Indian House. On one of my western car trips, I had stopped at a gallery which featured Native American art. Everything was forgettable—except for one particular portrait of a beautiful Native American woman. It seemed to jump off the wall. What made it so special was her evocative expression. It was positively luminous, yet full of sadness and longing.

"There's a story behind that painting," the gallery owner said.

That didn't surprise me. Everything about my life seemed to have a story.

"That was painted by Jim Abeita. It's a picture of his first wife. About a year later she was killed in a car accident."

It seemed Abeita's wife was the source of his inspiration. Soon after her death, he plunged into depression and alcoholism, and his paintings seemed to become mechanical, falling back on Native American clichés such as warriors, horses, teepees. But the paintings done before his wife's death were subtle and filled with mystery.

I discovered that Abeita had remarried and briefly recaptured the subtlety of his earlier work only to have his second wife die. Once again he fell into despair and lost his artistic inspiration. Thus, there were two times in his life when this artist's special talent flourished, and I began to put out the word that I was looking for paintings done in these periods. Occasionally, the phone would ring, and a dealer would say, "Allen, I've found one for you!"

My ambition was to display Abeita's paintings and other art works in unique ways in the Indian House. For the door to the den, I put a Navajo rug between two panes of glass; a local artist made original mosaics for the kitchen counters and tabletop; the benches were covered with tooled leather and a brass banister with crossed arrows lined the curving stone staircase.

As I looked at my progress in decorating the Indian House, I felt I needed an additional element to pull everything together. In my travels I met an artist named Thorny Harby who specialized in painting Native American scenes. I invited him to come live on the ranch in return for doing some paintings for me. Over the next year or so, he painted original western scenes on canvases as well as on every cabinet door in the house.

When I was done, I felt I had achieved a balance between a house and a museum—the integration of art into everyday life. You could be in the house for a week and still find something new to look at. But at the same time it was not overwhelmingly big or sterile like a museum.

During this period Julie and Billy came to visit me, and when they saw the ranch, they fell in love with it. It was so different than the New York apartment they were cooped up in. They learned to ride horses and watched the cowboys rope and brand cattle at our yearly roundup. It was an absolute paradise for them, and they didn't want to leave.

After consulting with Marilyn (and the lawyers, of course), it was decided that the kids would come to live with me. So, well into my sixties, I became a practicing father again. I was constantly driving Billy and Julie here and there for classes, to see the orthodontist, or to visit friends. As I found myself waiting for them to finish whatever it was they were doing, I began to realize how lonely I had become. I had always been a loner, without a circle of close friends, and now I was paying the price.

Sometimes, when I was waiting for one of the kids, I would drop into a coffee shop in Carmel called The Broken Egg. A group of locals hung out there talking about the day's news or local events. On several of my visits, I noticed an intriguing lady with a quick wit, a ready smile—and no wedding ring.

One morning I ventured into The Broken Egg while Billy was at an improv class and Julie was having a set of braces installed. It turned out that no one was there except the lady I had my eye on. We began talking and I was amazed at how easily the conversation flowed. She seemed to be able to pick up on any topic I raised.

I learned that her name was Anne Flynn and that she had never married, possibly because of a tragedy that occurred in her teenage years. Her father had been an officer in the Navy on the ship that delivered the A-bomb which was dropped on Hiroshima. As his ship headed back to the U.S., only days before the end of the war, it was torpedoed by the Japanese and he was killed. Anne's mother never really recovered from the shock, and Anne observed the effects of loving someone so deeply. Anne devoted her life to working and helping raise her sister's three children.

At this time I was producing "Candid Camera" specials, and I needed to be in L.A. for the shooting. I rented an unusual house in Nichols Canyon, in the Hollywood Hills, to use as a location for one special. At one end of the house was a two-story circular room which looked out on a thick jungle of a garden. The property was divided by a stream which became a river during the winter rains. When the "Candid Camera" taping was over, I found I'd grown attached to the place. And so I bought it.

I was once again in the position of looking for someone to help me remodel a house. This time I found a young man with a remarkable story, and I'm pleased to say he's still working for me today.

Born in El Salvador, Vladimir Rivera fled his war-ravaged homeland in 1980, and escaped to the U.S. where he began earning money to bring his family here. In 1987, he returned to El Salvador and literally carried his aged mother on his back through the jungles to freedom.

Vladimir either knew, or quickly learned, how to do almost everything. The biggest project we completed was to create a traditional Japanese garden. This involved designing and building several ornate bridges across the stream that flowed through my property. Vladimir labored long and hard to complete this garden, and it provides me with many hours of pleasure as a refuge from the noise and artificial clutter of Los Angeles.

Soon after buying the Nichols Canyon house, I fell into a pattern of spending weekdays in Los Angeles, then flying up to Carmel to be with Anne for the weekends. While our relationship deepened, I was simply too disenchanted with marriage to try it again.

For the past ten years, Anne and I have taken trips to many corners of the world. And wherever we go, we meet people who enjoy "Candid Camera" and want to tell me about their favorite gag or how much the show means to them.

On one trip to Africa, we had to change planes in a dusty airport that was 500 miles from anything Americans would call civilization. The terminal was nothing more than a tin shack, run by one lonely man. But as he checked my ticket, his face lit up. "You're Allen Funt!" he exclaimed. "I love 'Candid Camera!'"

With my ranch in full operation, my various new houses renovated, and my life filled with Anne and visits from my children, I was able to devote my professional interest to what was developing as a big business for "Candid Camera": the making of the network specials.

A Web of Words

I ONCE asked a man, "Where can I buy some scruples?" The guy thought it over and answered, "I haven't seen any since I was a kid."

Confusion over the meaning of certain words seems to be a universal human flaw—something we have happily underscored in numerous "Candid Camera" sequences. Some words are easily confused because of their similarity to other words. But a few words cause trouble because they sound as if they should mean something that they don't.

Among my favorites: retroactive. We stopped a man on his way into a drugstore. "I wouldn't go in there," I cautioned. "I think these people are very retroactive." His reply, "Oh, they're having labor trouble." Another fellow was stopped before entering an elevator and told that the car was retroactive. "I know what you mean," he said. "It stops with a jerk."

In *What Do You Say to a Naked Lady?*, I presented a middle-aged woman with a list of words and asked her to categorize each as either "clean" or "dirty." Here are her opinions:

Torque. "I think that's clean."

Horehound. "Dirty."

Seersucker. "Dirty."

Titillate. "That's dirty."

Thespian. "That's dirty too."

Fugue. "Clean."

Matriculate. "Dirty."

In this situation, five of seven perfectly "clean" words were viewed as "dirty," simply because of their sounds. Twenty years later, my son Peter did a piece for our Playboy series in which he pretended to take a survey about airline safety. The question: "Would it be proper for a pilot to ejaculate if there was still a chance to save the plane?" Here, a sexual term was perceived as nonsexual because of its sound and the context in which it was used.

Subject #1: "It would be proper if it doesn't bother the passengers."

Subject #2: "I didn't know there were planes where you could do that. A fighter plane, maybe."

Subject #3: "As long as a sign would go on telling people to fasten their seat belts."

Subject #4: "Am I on 'Candid Camera'?"

Rip-Offs, Spin-Offs and Specials

I was on location shooting a special for CBS when I got an urgent call from my son, Peter. We usually shot the specials as a team, Peter working on the East Coast, while I worked out of Los Angeles. Naturally, I assumed the call was about our project. I was wrong.

"I just heard there's another rip-off coming out," Peter said.

I started to say I was too busy to drop everything and pay attention to yet another "Candid Camera" imitator. Over the years many people tried to copy our show. Invariably, when they found out how hard this format is to produce, they failed and disappeared.

"Listen to me," Peter said. "Listen to the title of this show. It's called 'Hidden Video.'"

What he said gradually sank in—and my anger began to build. Most of our earlier imitators had the decency at least to

189

appear as if they had a new and improved idea. But the Fox network not only stole our concept, they came as close as they could to using our title. If you sat in a room with a group of programmers and decided to do an obvious knock-off of "Candid Camera," the most synonymous name would be "Hidden Video."

"I really think we have to do something about this," Peter said.

"So do I, but..." I didn't finish as I recalled all the other times I had tried to go after imitators and had come away with little or no compensation. But then I thought of that damned title again, "Hidden Video."

"Let's find out more about the show first," I said. "Then we'll decide how to handle it."

As Peter tried to track down a preview copy of the show, I returned to work on the special.

Since 1987, we have produced fourteen of these specials for CBS. And, like the other chapters in the "Candid Camera" story, the specials include their own joys and frustrations. The joy is that we have the distinction of producing prime-time shows, devoted to single subjects, with generous budgets. The frustration is that CBS doesn't seem to view "Candid Camera" with the high regard it once had. While our specials have been used for important "sweeps" periods, they are often inadequately promoted and shuffled into poor time slots.

In fairness to CBS, television has changed dramatically since the sixties. Programmers now cater to shorter attention spans and believe that audiences will not tolerate a buildup to a climax. They want everything to be so visually gripping that even stupefied viewers flipping the channel will be hooked by a single glimpse of what they see. As the eighties churned forward and cable gave birth to the MTV generation, the competitive atmosphere became more intense, and the demand for faster, punchier scenes became greater.

My own opinion of television has steadily declined to the point where I only watch public TV, sports, and the news. It seems that too many shows are tasteless and exploitative.

These terms could have been used to describe the Fox program "Hidden Video." Peter called me back when he had located a demo copy of the show at a Manhattan advertising agency. The demo had been distributed in hopes of preselling commercials.

Peter was angered and amazed by what he saw on the tape. In the first sequence, a couple was shown being tricked at a gas station, then informed that they were on "Hidden Video." The couple went through all the hysteria of typical "Candid Camera" subjects, screaming "We're on television! Oh my God, I can't believe it!"

Purely by coincidence, Peter happened to recognize the two people in this scene as former classmates of his at the University of Denver. He knew that they had moved to Los Angeles after graduation and were working as improv actors. In other words, not only was "Hidden Video" a poor imitation of "Candid Camera," but it was a fraud—they were hiring little-known actors to pretend to be unsuspecting people caught by hidden cameras.

I have always been outraged by charges that "Candid Camera" scenes were faked. Ever since that day on the golf course when we made a believer of Mr. Woods, we have strived to protect our credibility and the honesty of our format. If "Hidden Video" was allowed to be broadcast, I felt it might damage the future of "Candid Camera." I called my lawyer.

I wish I could conclude this story by saying that justice was served. Instead, our request for a temporary restraining order to block the Fox broadcast was denied. When the show had its debut, the specific scenes we knew to have been faked were removed and the series was called "Totally Hidden Video." (I wondered if the title was modified to disguise the similarity to "Candid Camera.") In the credits, they even had the audacity to list someone as the "creator" of the show.

After weeks of legal maneuvering, during which the case was covered extensively in the media (providing valuable publicity for Fox's show), the judge decided that "Totally Hidden Video" would be allowed to continue, although I was awarded $150,000. When I added up the legal fees, they came to $175,000. The Fox program changed hosts and stage sets about a half-dozen times, then was canceled.

I could have told any would-be imitator that "Candid Camera" was difficult to copy. I myself had been trying to "imitate" it for years—with spin-offs. My first attempt resulted in a short-lived series back in 1963 called "Tell it to the Camera." This was the opposite of "Candid Camera" in that the camera was completely exposed. We put a camera crew in a van, traveling across the country to shopping centers and other public spots where people were invited to speak their minds in front of the camera.

The show never really came together, and it was canceled by CBS after thirteen episodes. This was mainly my fault since I was spread so thin producing "Candid Camera."

Years later, I interested another network in letting me try the "Tell it to the Camera" concept again, but with one change: the dialogue took place in unusual locations. For the demo tape, we went to a maximum security prison where the power of the format was underscored by the comments from one inmate. In a way which was both frightening and funny, the felon began to speak his mind.

"Honey," he said, apparently addressing his ex-wife, "I just want you to know, I still love you." He paused and continued flatly, "But I know you'll never forgive me for killing both your parents that night..."

Another spin-off I tried, in 1985, was a children's version of "Candid Camera" for NBC called "Candid Kids." My cohost was Nancy McKeon of "The Facts of Life." We had a kids' "Talking Mailbox" and a few gags in which child actors pulled the tricks.

Years earlier we had used a child to help fool adults. We set up a scene in which taxi drivers were sent to a doctor's office, ostensibly for an insurance exam. As they arrived and got ready for the exam, the nurse told them, "I don't want you to get nervous about this, but the doctor is quite young." The cabbies would nod agreeably. But the nurse would be very insistent, "No, I mean he's very young." And at that moment the "doctor" would walk in, and the cabbies would see he was all of about eight years old. He even had a little stool to stand on so he could listen to each patient's chest. After the "doctor" left, one cab driver said to the nurse, "I'm going right to the phone and tell our daughter to start my grandson in medical school—today!"

In addition to these domestic spin-offs, we have licensed the "Candid Camera" format in several foreign countries. The first such deal came about after I learned there was someone in England doing a show just like ours. Since our lawyers believed there was little we could do to stop it, I decided to sell the British company a formal license to do a version of our show.

The producer of the English series was Jonathan Routh and his only claim to fame was a book called *A Guide to the Loo's of London* ("loo" being English slang for a bathroom). Jonathan wanted to produce the show, dream up the ideas, and act in the scenes. In other words, he wanted to become the Allen Funt of

England. He set about to copy me in every way he could, but with one big exception—he was ten times as audacious.

I decided I should make a trip over and visit Jonathan before we closed the licensing deal. He picked me up at the airport in an old Rolls Royce convertible roadster. It started to rain, but instead of putting up the top, he drove across London holding an umbrella over our heads. When we got to his office, I found it was located behind a fruit store. You had to duck behind hanging bunches of bananas and jump over crates of oranges to get to his office door. None of this was for a "Candid Camera" sketch; this was just the way he lived his life.

There is a silliness to the English sense of humor that Jonathan wanted to exploit, and he did so in some outrageous ways which I would never have dared try. In one particularly unbelievable piece, he dressed in an astronaut's suit. He then stopped two plump English ladies and persuaded them that he needed help getting airborne. He told them to take the other end of a rope tied around his waist and run as fast as they could until he was pulled into orbit. It was quite a sight to see the three of them—two English matrons and a guy in a space suit— puffing down the street as fast as they could go.

In recent years the foreign market has continued to grow, and I've been able to sell the rights to "Candid Camera" in some of the most unlikely places. We signed deals in Greece and Morocco and, if you can believe it, in the midst of all the turmoil in that part of the world, someone bought the rights to produce "Candid Camera" in Yugoslavia.

Before shooting the pilot for "Candid Kids," we did an hour-long NBC special marking "Candid Camera's 35th Anniversary." The special did well in the ratings, and NBC invited us to do more shows on specific themes. A few years later, we moved to

CBS and the list of specials grew to include sports, dining out, cars, money, Christmas, doctors and other topics.

With the first of the specials, I stepped in front of the camera once again. I had been on camera for the syndicated run in the seventies, and to a lesser degree for the Playboy series. But I hadn't been on network television for perhaps a decade—and I was afraid I would find out that the public had forgotten me. I never considered myself a celebrity, so I was always surprised—and tickled—when someone stopped to tell me how much they liked the show or asked me to sign an autograph. I feel foolish admitting it, but I enjoyed the special treatment I got from my audience, and the thought that my popularity might have evaporated was frightening.

My anxiety was triggered by an incident in a Beverly Hills restaurant. A man noticed me and said to his wife, "You know who this is? He used to be Allen Funt!"

So, as we approached production of the first special, I was nervous about how the public would respond to me. In the sequences, my appearance was disguised with a baseball hat and glasses. Still, although years had passed, my voice often tipped people off to who I was. I realized then that while my hair went from gray to white and my face aged, my voice remained almost unchanged. All those kids who grew up watching "Candid Camera" back in the sixties were now adults, and my voice, with its characteristic Brooklyn accent, was preserved in their memories.

A person's voice is an audible signature. We used this idea as the basis of a gag involving the comic Jim Morris—and we came to hire him for the show in an unusual way. Peter was filming a sequence for a special called "Eat, Eat, Eat" in a diner in Norwalk, Connecticut. Posing as a waiter, Peter drew customers' attention to the "Extra Special"—a turkey sandwich for only sixty-five cents. But when it arrived, diners found two lonely pieces of bread sparsely populated with slices of turkey. They also learned that to have the sandwich accompanied by cole slaw was a dollar extra. Ketchup was sixty-five cents extra. Even a packet of sugar was a nickel extra. Eventually they realized the "Extra Special" was so named because anything extra cost extra.

Many customers ordered the "Extra Special," and many became perturbed when Peter informed them of the cost of the extras. Unbeknownst to Peter, Jim Morris, the skillful impressionist, happened to be in the diner that day, seated at a nearby table where he observed the whole thing.

After Jim watched us work on one exasperated couple, he tried to come to their aid. Before he could barge in and ruin the scene, he was intercepted by one of our crew (we always have someone stand by to keep onlookers away). When he found out it was a gag, he laughed harder than anyone else. Afterwards he said he had always been a fan of the show and would love to be on it. Since his specialty was doing impressions of famous people, we came up with an idea that made good use of his talents.

We hired temporary secretaries to answer phones in an office that specialized in catering elegant banquets. We instructed the workers that an important event was being arranged and some celebrities might be calling to give their special recipes. Then we left them alone. The phone rang, and the secretaries found themselves talking to then-President George Bush (imitated by Jim Morris, of course). The next time the phone rang, it was Dan Rather or some other celebrity. When the boss (also played by Jim) returned to the room, the secretaries would say, "You wouldn't believe who just called!" It worked perfectly because Jim's voices were so convincing.

Unlike the weekly TV show, these "Candid Camera" specials are done only when a network gives us an order. About fourteen sequences are needed to fill an hour, and it usually takes three weeks of shooting and another two weeks of editing to complete an hourlong program.

I say "usually" because the flexible time schedule that distinguishes a special from a weekly series is both a blessing and a curse. Since "Candid Camera" is based on the unpredictability of human responses, rather than a planned script, who's to say that an extra day—or an extra week—of shooting might not yield a funnier result? The only signal for us to stop working is the network's insistence that it is time to go on the air. Often, when one of our specials is delayed because of a change in the network schedule, we keep shooting, spending more time and money in search of a funnier slice of life.

One such delay had Peter and crew traveling in North Carolina on March 5, 1989. On previous weekends, they had photographed the humorous antics of auto-racing fans at tracks in Virginia and Georgia. But I felt they needed one more trip to one more racecourse. While Peter was shooting, his wife Amy went into labor in New York, and my first grandchild, Stephanie, was born. It reminded me of that night in 1947 when I was so wrapped up in editing "Candid Microphone" that Evelyn almost didn't make it to the hospital in time for Peter's birth.

As the specials rolled on in the nineties, it was gratifying to discover that audiences still enjoyed our format, and critics, after decades of indecision, seemed to be warming to our efforts. In 1990, *Variety* wrote: "The latest new 'Candid Camera' specials seem to be getting funnier. With Allen and Peter Funt leading the way, the show has begun to invest more time in skits and concentrate on lengthier 'Camera' antics, which are much more suitable for this format." Reviews like that certainly fly in the face of network assertions that only brief, snappy scenes can please an MTV-conditioned audience.

A year later, *Variety* added that the specials were "bringing back the energy of the show's earlier years." And the *New York Daily News* noted, "For some crazy reason, Allen Funt's 'Candid Camera' manages to hold up. One would think by now people would not be so easily trapped."

Producing two or three prime-time specials each year is perhaps the most enjoyable—and lucrative—situation a producer can find himself in. Why anyone would allow a flash of greed to disrupt this, I'll never know, but that's what happened in 1991 when I allowed the King World company to produce a daily, syndicated version of "Candid Camera."

I can only say that, although I agreed to all the terms presented to me by King World's lawyers, I was led to believe that I would have some meaningful input into the creation of the gags and the format of the show. As soon as the ink was dry on my signature, King World began making a show which was a complete embarrassment. The choice of stunts, the tone of the show, and the selection of Dom DeLuise as host were counter to everything I tried to suggest. This project, although authorized, amounted to one of the worst "Candid Camera" rip-offs ever. I was relieved when the show went off the air in a relatively short time.

I've always felt that while "Candid Camera" is successful, it is misunderstood. The fact that so many others have tried to copy our format and failed is proof of this. Even people who watch "Candid Camera" and enjoy it sometimes feel that it is cruel and that we are in business to make fools of people. I'm very sensitive to these charges because I know how hard we try to avoid cruelty. And yet, as I discovered early on, there is an element of cruelty in all humor. We try to offset this by turning our subjects into heroes. Yes, we've tricked them, but we want to praise them for letting us all watch, enjoy, and learn from the scene.

While I sometimes complain about being misunderstood, occasionally I encounter a critic who hits the mark. During the time of the "Hidden Video" lawsuit, I happened to see a review of our special, "Funny Money," written by Ray Richmond in California's *Orange County Register*. He praised the special, but more importantly, he summarized the differences between "Candid Camera" and its imitators:

"'Candid Camera' is further blessed with a quaint dignity, a gentleness, that's sorely lacking from the Fox Broadcasting rip-off 'Totally Hidden Video.' Whereas the mean-spirited 'Hidden Video' exists simply to embarrass people, 'Candid Camera' is really more a celebration of human nature. The folks caught by the hidden camera aren't played for fools but rather as people on the other end of a spirited practical joke. There's a difference. That distinction allows you to tune in tonight—and laugh—without feeling guilty."

Types of Reactions

FOR all the aggravation that the Fox program "Totally Hidden Video" caused me, there was one particularly dull element of the show that I found hilarious. No matter what they tried, they could never do a successful "reveal." Obviously, they wouldn't dare use the word "smile." And the phrase, "You're on 'Hidden Video,'" usually brought blank stares. It pleased me to envision tormented Fox editors snipping out the inevitable, "You mean 'Candid Camera?'" or, "Where's Allen Funt?"

Forty-five years ago we, too, had to do a bit of explaining before unsuspecting people understood our reveals. But gradually the enormous power of television actually helped to condition millions of viewers about what was expected if they should ever hear the words, "Smile! You're on 'Candid Camera.'" I believe that this conditioning actually gave many of our subjects the subconscious inclination to hug me or collapse while yelping in disbelief. That has become the most common reaction among people caught by the "Candid Camera," but there are a few other recurrent reactions that we have observed.

1. GO NUMB. Some people are so amazed by our reveal that they seem to go into a state of shock. We've received letters explaining that the truth took several hours to sink in, after which the subjects were usually delighted.

2. "I KNEW IT!" A surprising number of people respond by saying, "I knew it all along"—even though they didn't. This seems to be a defensive attempt to show that they can't be easily duped.

3. RELIEF. Often our subjects are relieved to learn that the predicaments we have placed them in are not real (say, mirrors in a wig shop that break when women look in them).

4. DISAPPOINTMENT. But some folks are sad to learn that a situation is not real, and simply the result of our staff's ingenuity (a slot machine that pays off every time the handle is pulled).

5. ANGER. A small percentage of people, most of whom willingly sign releases, express anger upon learning they were caught by the "Candid Camera." I'm not sure why; the anger is rarely focused. I assume that these people object to being tricked or resent the intrusion in their day.

6. DISBELIEF. When told he's on television, this subject says, "No." When shown the camera and microphone, he says, "You're kidding me." When asked to sign a release, he does so willingly—but still thinks the gag is that we're *pretending* to be "Candid Camera," not that we really *are* "Candid Camera." I often wonder what this person thinks when he finally sees himself on TV. I suppose he figures we've hired an actor to impersonate him.

The Top Ten

No matter where I go, or who I meet, the same questions always seem to be tossed at me. Have you ever been sued? (A few times, but never for much money.) Has anyone ever caught you with a hidden camera? (No. But it has always scared me that if caught I wouldn't be a good sport.) When did you start losing your hair? (Too long ago to worry about it.)

But more than anything else, people want to know: what's your all-time favorite "Candid Camera" sequence? Well, that's like asking a mother to choose a favorite from among her kids. Except in my case, we've shot tens of thousands of "Candid Camera" pieces over nearly forty-five years. On two occasions, when producing anniversary specials, I've tried to identify the "best" by category. For example, many of our memorable gags involved telephones; quite a few featured cars; lunch counters are fertile territory for us, as is any local nursery school.

In constructing this Top Ten list recently, I tried to consider which sequences were the funniest and most memorable, as well as those that broke new ground in our people-watching pursuits. Here's my list:

1. THE TALKING MAILBOX (1954)

I've mentioned earlier that this simple piece on a Manhattan street corner has endured as perhaps the most memorable "Candid Camera" sequence ever. I'm not sure why. All we did was put a speaker in a mailbox and draw passersby into conversation by asking, "Have you seen the mail truck? I haven't been emptied yet."

I do know that, like so many other bits of good fortune in my life, the climax of the scene—in which our subject is joined by another passerby for whom the mailbox refuses to talk— happened completely by accident. Just as our subject pleaded, "Here's another guy that don't believe there's someone in the box. Speak up!" our soundman kicked the plug leading to the speaker in the mailbox. My buddy Dick Christman actually continued talking as the voice of the mailbox, but the silence that went out over the air was golden.

2. THE RESTROOM (1958)

All we needed for this sequence was a small executive clothes closet in the lobby of a Manhattan movie theater and a sign which we pasted on the door: RESTROOM.

As in so many of my favorites, hardly a word is spoken as one frustrated moviegoer after another steps in, parts the hanging clothes, and exits in dismay. Maybe it was because a few members of our staff occasionally stepped out of the closet, drying their hands; maybe it was because folks who dash out of a movie seeking relief are easily miffed—whatever it was, the expressions we photographed that day were among the most memorable in forty-five years of "Candid Camera." And for a while we couldn't show it.

NBC's censors told us that a piece about a bathroom was unacceptable. They cited a section in the program practices manual that forbade jokes about "agencies"—the censors' own delicate term for restrooms.

No matter how vehemently we argued, our innocent few minutes of silent film were barred from the air. Then luck again came our way. One of NBC's biggest stars, Jack Paar, got into a much-publicized feud over using the term "water closet" on the "Tonight" show. The press was critical of NBC, and after that the censors loosened up and decided maybe "restroom" wasn't such a nasty term after all. We aired the film and it became such a favorite that we used it over and over again.

3. FACING THE REAR (1962)

Many of our hidden-camera gags have proved useful to educators and psychologists studying human behavior. Of course, we never set out with such lofty goals. On this autumn day in 1962, we simply wanted to find out what would happen if an elevator passenger discovered that while he faced forward, everyone else in the car turned and faced the rear.

As we watched from our hiding place, we were flabbergasted at the results. One person after another bowed to group pressure and reversed his or her position. Indeed, as the day wore on, we influenced passengers to face the left, the right, and, in the case of one fellow, to remove his hat and then put it back on, simply because that is what our staff members did with their hats.

4. CINDERELLA (1963)

I've been charmed by thousands of kids over the years but none was more delightful than a seven-year-old named Debbie. In typical form, I arrived at Debbie's school without a clue about the direction our conversations might take. Then, magically, this shy young lady mentioned "Cinderella" and burst out of her shell.

Soon, I was Prince Charming as Debbie played the title role. With paper party hats as props, we danced the night away. Then I mentioned something about the clock striking twelve. "I gotta go, I gotta go," she screamed. Instinctively, I grabbed a loop on the back of her dress to hold her back, while begging her to stay. "I gotta go," she squealed again. I kept holding onto her. "Please, Cinderella, can't I have just one more dance?"

Finally, with a mighty tug to break free, she exclaimed, "I'll be back tomorrow!" And with that, she was gone.

That day, Debbie taught me two important lessons. First, such is the wonder of youth, that reality and fantasy are often inseparable. Without a moment's preparation, this little girl actually became Cinderella before our camera.

The other thing I learned that day is that with "Candid Camera," you have only one chance to capture a charming moment. Midway in our scene—which ran about four minutes—was an interruption that never appeared in the edited sequence.

Just as Debbie made a particularly sweet remark, a technician hiding in the next room knocked over some metal film cans. At the sound of the crash, I turned and bellowed, "Quiet back there!" Then, trying to compose myself and salvage her comment, I turned back to Debbie and said, "I'm sorry, my darling. Would you please say that again?"

"Sure," said Debbie. "Quiet back there!"

5. CAR WITHOUT A MOTOR (1960)

Dorothy Collins did so many successful automobile gags for us in the sixties that we gave her the on-air nickname Crash Collins. By far the best of all these stunts was the "Car Without a Motor."

As you read earlier, filling station attendants were incredulous when faced with a car whose engine compartment contained nothing but daylight, and a lady motorist whose only concern was that it be "fixed quickly so my husband doesn't get angry."

The story behind this story is that sometimes on "Candid Camera" we try to go too far. During the first few takes, my son Peter—a teen back then—was dressed as an auto mechanic and leaped out from under the hood when the unsuspecting attendants looked inside. We had hoped to persuade the subjects that this nutty woman had driven off from the previous station while a mechanic was still working on her engine. It never worked. The stimulation in this version of the scene was so jarring that the subjects were literally paralyzed in astonishment—thus no outward reaction. When we toned things down, simply revealing nothing under the hood, the subjects were startled but, fortunately, not quite speechless.

6. THE TALKING HORSE (1963)

At Hialeah Racetrack in Florida, we found a section where visitors on a bus tour were allowed to inspect the horses in their stalls. All the horses in one particular row were named "Pitt"-something. Why? "I'm from Pittsburgh," said the trainer. "That's why." He agreed to lend us a gentle thoroughbred named Pittpena.

I wired her up with a little speaker, and as tourists passed by her stall, Pittpena, in my voice, would go, "Pssssssssst." Several friendly people stopped to talk. Folks seemed to enjoy the pleasures of her conversation (in my voice).

Soon a nice fellow came by. He turned out to be a judge from California.

"Do you want a tip on the second race?" Pittpena whispered to the judge. "I'm not in the race, so you don't have to worry. But I have a friend who is."

The judge smiled, nonplused, and listened carefully.

"Can I trust you not to spread it around too much?"

The judge agreed. Then he looked at Pittpena. "Is it all right to tell it to my wife?"

Pittpena said yes. "I think the horse you ought to bet on in the second race is Apocalypse."

The judge started to write it down. Then he turned to the horse and asked, "How do you spell it?"

7. THE UNANSWERABLE TELEPHONE (1962)

Telephones are marvelous tools for the "Candid Camera." We've had squirting phones, smelly phones, phone booths that rose eight feet into the air, phone booths that sank into the ground—we even trained an elephant to interrupt people as they spoke on a pay phone. Aside from the fact that people often find phones frustrating, they are useful props for us because people on the phone tend to stay in one spot, making it easy to take their picture.

My favorite phone gag took place in a flower shop, where we placed two identical phones on the counter. While the clerk steps out, a lady customer is asked to answer the phone. Soon it rings, but no matter how hard she tries, she cannot lift the receiver, which we have screwed to the base of the phone.

And with that we got a true classic. The piece that ran on the air lasted several minutes and consisted of nothing other than a ringing phone and a determined woman. She banged it. She tugged at it. She repeatedly picked up the other phone, just in case that might somehow stop the ringing. And several times she lifted the entire instrument and shouted at it, "Just a minute!"

The beauty of the sequence is that it goes on as long as it does. I sometimes worry that today's frenetic TV editing would destroy a piece that builds and builds with each jarring ring of the phone.

8. THE TRAMPOLINE (1966)

While some stunts, like "The Unanswerable Phone," were remarkably simple to set up, others were painfully elaborate. In a Manhattan gymnasium, temporary secretaries were hired to answer the phone and keep an eye on things as people came in to test the equipment. We used the services of the world's champion trampolinist at the time, George Hery, posing as a customer. By constructing a false ceiling in the gym, we were able to have George test the trampoline, then bounce right up through the ceiling and disappear!

As I mentioned earlier, sometimes a shocking image leaves people completely speechless. In this case, it really didn't matter. Each time George flew through the ceiling, and pieces of tile and plaster dust poured down, our subjects spoke volumes with their expressions. It was one of the toughest "Candid Camera" sequences we ever did but certainly one of the best.

9. GOLDIE (1975)

It's a showbiz axiom that you're asking for trouble by working with little children or animals. But photographing kids has been perhaps the brightest part of my career and, frankly, we've never hired an animal for "Candid Camera" who failed to get a laugh. The best was a small collie named Goldie.

Goldie's trainer came to my office one day, trying to interest me in his dog's latest trick. At the sound of a ringing phone, Goldie would walk over to a typewriter, pull out the paper, and drop it in a wastebasket. Why anyone would teach an animal this particular trick I'll never know, but here's how we put Goldie to work on "Candid Camera."

A temporary secretary comes into my office. She's told about the difficulty in getting talented animals for our TV show. I ask her to take a letter...

Dear John,

The dog you loaned me was not right. In fact, this is one of the stupidest dogs I've ever seen. The sooner we get rid of her the better, because I can't stand her. Thanks anyhow.

Signed, Allen

Goldie is sitting in the room as the secretary starts to type. Then, the phone rings, giving Goldie her cue. While the secretary answers the call, Goldie scampers over to the typewriter, yanks out the paper, and drops it in the wastebasket.

The puzzled secretary starts with a new sheet of paper—
and another call comes in. After several tries, I return to the
room, demanding the finished letter.

Says our Candid star: "You won't believe this, but..."

10. JAMESTOWN PITCHER (1991)

Over the years we've developed several House Rules for our
hidden-camera work. For instance, we don't target a single
individual for a gag—the odds are too slim that the person
would be interesting or funny. We usually photograph twenty
or thirty people for a stunt, then select the two or three best for
airing.

Another no-no for us is the use of multiple cameras. Even
when the budget allows more than one camera, I've always felt
strongly about sticking with just one. At best, "Candid Camera"
has a through-the-keyhole quality—something that just doesn't
work when the scene cuts from one camera to another.

But all rules have their exceptions, and our visit to a minor
league baseball stadium in Jamestown, New York, broke all the
rules. With the blessing of the parent club, the Montreal Expos,
and help from the Jamestown Expos catcher, we confounded
pitcher Bob Baxter so he couldn't throw a single pitch. Catcher
Dan Hargus gave Baxter strange signals he'd never seen before.
With my son Peter as the home-plate umpire urging him on,
Baxter stood on the mound for at least ten minutes, shaking his
head and unable to throw any type of pitch.

Not only did we catch Baxter, we also fooled the players on
both teams, several thousand spectators, and the broadcasters
from a local radio station who tried in vain to explain the delay
to their listeners. When it came time for a reveal, the public

address announcer told everyone to "Smile! You and the Expos are all on 'Candid Camera.'"

Of course, if we had failed that night in Jamestown, we would have had to move to another city and thousands of dollars would have been lost. To reduce the danger of a technical foul-up, we did use two cameras and four microphones.

As our sequence ended, Peter went out to the mound and told Bob Baxter, "You're one of the nicest guys we've ever had on 'Candid Camera,' although you're shaking like a leaf!" Though poor Baxter had not thrown a single pitch, that night we felt like we had really hit one out of the park.

*   *   *

In compiling this Top Ten, I found myself creating a separate list of sequences that never seemed to get the attention I think they deserved. So, here is my Top Ten list of "unsung" favorites.

1. DELAWARE CLOSED TODAY (1965)

We've done many sequences centering on authority. On a highway, it need not be a police officer in uniform. It can be nothing more than a man with a hard hat, a sign, and a tone of authority. That's all we needed to convince motorists that the state of Delaware was closed for the day. The explanation was that Delaware was crowded, and we suggested that motorists use New Jersey.

2. THE UPSIDE-DOWN ROOM (1962)

Without a doubt, this was the toughest stunt we've ever tried. At the Seattle World's Fair, we built a room that was completely upside down. All the furniture—desk, chair, lamp, etc.—was bolted to a false ceiling. Papers were glued onto the desk and inside the upside-down wastebasket. Pictures on the wall were inverted. And my son Peter, supported only by a seat belt and blind confidence that his father knew what he was doing, hung upside down behind the desk, talking with visitors to the fair. My only regret is that people didn't say very much. Again, they seemed paralyzed by the unbelievability of what they were seeing.

3. THREE KIDS, ONE CONE (1961)

How would three kindergarten pupils handle a single ice cream cone? When our Bob Schwartz arranged it, he seated a boy between two girls. Bob gave the boy a cone and told the girls to be patient while he went for theirs. Almost immediately the two females began badgering the little guy in the middle for one bite after another. Finally, when the cone was finished, Bob returned with two more. "Can I have a bite?" the boy asked meekly. "We're not going to share with you," shot back one girl. "You already had yours!"

4. BEAUT-O-MATIC (1990)

For a CBS special we built a "machine" called the Beaut-o-matic, a rather crude contraption that did little more than test our subjects' gullibility. One by one we brought professional beauticians to a showroom where Peter was demonstrating this unique device. As the subjects looked on, Peter would shove a young lady (our actress) in one end of the machine; a minute later she would roll out the other end with a new hairstyle, makeup and manicure! Out of eleven beauticians photographed that day, all but one believed that the Beaut-o-matic lived up to our claims. And not a single subject guessed the

truth: that what they were "seeing"—and therefore believing—
was actually one actress going into the machine and her identical twin sister coming out.

5. BOUND AND GAGGED (1962)

I'm usually pretty good at predicting what people will do when
caught in our setups. But this particular stunt in May of 1962
fooled me completely. Deliverymen arrived at my office with a
small lunch order, only to find me tied with rope at the wrists
and ankles and my mouth gagged. Not one fellow offered to
help with my obvious predicament. The most courteous comment I got was, "If you'd like, I can come back later."

6. BLANK PICKETS (1965)

In front of a vacant lot in New York City, our Joey Faye and several cohorts carried picket signs and handed out leaflets. The
catch? The signs and the leaflets were completely blank. "We
need your support," exclaimed Joey as people came by. Several
folks pledged support; a few even picked up signs and joined
the picket line.

7. DISAPPEARING SPOON (1961)

Elliot Joslin created many extraordinary props for us, but sometimes the simplest were the best. Once, he cut the handles off
some spoons, then reattached them with cement that would
dissolve when the temperature reached 110 degrees. At a lunch
counter, people who ordered coffee got one of Elliot's spoons—
and we got a collection of the most bewildered expressions
ever seen on "Candid Camera."

8. JULIE AND MONEY (1972)

For my movie *Money Talks*, I decided to turn the hidden camera on my daughter Juliet, who at the time was five, going on twenty-five...

Allen: What do you think is more important, money or love?

Julie: Well, I think they are very important, but the most important thing in the whole wide world is your heart.

Allen: Your heart?

Julie: Yeah.

Allen: How did you figure that out?

Julie: Because your heart gives you the strength, and the love, and the blood to live with.

Allen: I see.

Julie: If you didn't have a heart, you wouldn't live, and the world wouldn't be the world.

Our movie wasn't very successful, but the poignant remarks by my daughter made a touching sequence that was repeated many times on "Candid Camera." Most memorable was her considered conclusion after many minutes of debate on whether money is a requisite for happiness: "I think rich is somehow better than poor."

9. MATH PROBLEM (1965)

Most adults have forgotten simple math, such as, "How many square feet in a square yard?" Here's our proof.

Subject #1: "I didn't know a square yard was measured by feet. I think it would be three times three times three. Twenty-seven square feet."

Subject #2: "Six."

Interviewer: "Six what?"

Subject: "Six this way and six that way. Thirty-six."

Subject #3: "Multiply your square yards by nine, and divide by three, and reverse."

Subject #4: "You've got three square yards divided by square feet, divided by a hundred and twenty-four inches, isn't it?"

10. FREE SAMPLES (1965)

In a supermarket I put out a platter of biscuits, with a sign: FREE—TAKE ONE. We waited until a shopper sampled one, then a clerk moved part of the display to reveal the entire sign: DOG BISCUITS, FREE—TAKE ONE. Soon a lady with a baby came along and took one biscuit for herself and fed another to the child. The rest of the sign was uncovered. She spit out her biscuit and turned to the baby. "Oh well," she said, "let him eat it. He can't read anyway."

Famous Faces

HAVING photographed more than a million unsuspecting people, the law of averages would seem to suggest that at least a few of them would happen to be celebrities. I know of three in a million.

In 1960, a youthful Robert Redford was carrying a bag of dirty laundry down Third Avenue in Manhattan, when he passed a toy store where we were filming. A member of our staff, failing to recognize Redford, ran out of the store and asked for help in blowing up a huge inflatable toy. As we photographed him, Redford became red-faced as he strained to inflate the thing—which was, of course, impossible.

After a while, Redford began to suspect that the lights were a bit too bright for a toy store. Then he spotted me, peeking from behind a curtain, and that was it.

Because of a problem with the Screen Actors Guild, we never used the Redford piece. Thirty-three years later, his office asked us for a copy of the sequence. Regrettably, we only save footage that has been used on the air.

We did save a piece from 1965 in which high school students in Livingston, New Jersey, met with their guidance counselor to hear results of standardized aptitude tests. The first fellow, nattily attired in shirt, tie, and dark sweater, listened confidently as the counselor reported: "Richard, I've gone through your test scores and your other records in school, and I've come to the very definite and firm conclusion that you would be perfectly suited for manual labor."

"You said, 'manual labor'?"

"Yes."

"That's all? Just manual labor?"

"Manual labor."

"Gee, I never thought I was suited for manual labor before. You mean no intelligence, just manual labor?"

At this point, Richard is squirming in his chair, rubbing his head, and laughing nervously. I don't know exactly what career path he had been planning to take, but I have to wonder what Richard's reaction might have been if the counselor had said, "You would be perfectly suited for comedy. You'll be a frequent guest with David Letterman; you'll also costar with Jamie Lee Curtis in a popular sitcom called 'Anything But Love.'"

What on earth would Richard Lewis have said to that?

Then there was the time we were shooting a piece in a photographic supply store in Phoenix. One man, at the rear of the store, was not involved in our stunt—but he was clearly identifiable on camera as Senator Barry Goldwater.

As our sequence unfolded in front of the store, Senator Goldwater was in the back, stuffing flashbulbs into his pockets. After the reveal, we cautiously approached him to explain what we were doing. To our surprise, he readily signed a release.

As he left, he announced, "Naturally, I'm planning to pay for these bulbs on the way out."

Laughing Matters

P lease hurry, Allen," said Anne as I fiddled with my tie for the third or fourth time. "I don't think this is the type of group that likes to be kept waiting."

We were in a lovely room at the Hyatt Regency in San Francisco on a mild Saturday night in April. The ballroom downstairs was filled to capacity, and I was eager to learn how my speech would be received by this special audience. As Anne and I moved out the door, I patted my coat pocket to be sure I had my glasses. They were on the kitchen table back in Pebble Beach.

So much of my life has seemed like material from a "Candid Camera" gag that I should have expected something like this. Fortunately, I've given hundreds of lectures over the years and never used a prepared text. Indeed, all fourteen of our network specials, including the intros, were completely ad lib.

Still, I did need to refer to a list of "Candid Camera" clips which I had brought for this occasion. But where could I find suitable glasses on a Saturday night, 110 miles from home?

Suddenly a crazy thought flashed through my mind. Why not check the hotel's lost and found to see if, by chance, there was a pair that fitted my prescription? I raced to the lobby, mumbled something about losing my glasses, and located a pair in the lost and found that I could actually read with.

A few minutes later, with someone else's lost glasses, I began my speech.

"The most successful 'Candid Camera' scenes work because of what psychologists call 'consonant dissonance.'" I paused and squinted past the stage lights at the audience. I could feel a laugh beginning and I let it grow.

"I'm told this means that people have a special problem when they are exposed to contradictory circumstances. In 'The Car Without a Motor,' our staff rolled a car downhill to a gas station." Laughter began to ripple through the audience. "When Dorothy Collins got out and told the attendant it wasn't running well, the attendant opened the hood and found the engine compartment was empty. So, on one hand the guy finds that the car has no motor; on the other hand, he just saw the damned thing pull in."

The audience erupted in laughter.

I had been surrounded by laughter all my life, but I was always amazed at its ability to unify a group. I felt as though I was being picked up on a wave of approval and swept along. And this laughter was special. It wasn't a hollow laugh track or the artificially induced laughter from a studio audience. This was the 1991 meeting of the Western Psychological Association —600 of the most renowned psychologists from the Western states and Hawaii meeting in San Francisco. And I was the keynote speaker, discussing the conclusions I'd reached about society, human behavior, and life, through making "Candid Camera."

There was a pleasing irony in the fact that while I was occasionally panned by the critics and labeled a Peeping Tom by the press, my work now found a devoted following among psychologists. What I created as pure entertainment was embraced by this group as valuable experimentation in human behavior. It was, oddly enough, a happy meeting of the couch and the camera.

When the laughter died down, I continued my speech.

"I've often been amazed at how difficult it is to provoke people while they are doing their jobs. I believe that people involved in making a living rarely find anything funny connected with their livelihood. It seems that all of us lose our sense of humor when we are doing our jobs."

I paused again and I could feel the crowd waiting for the example that was sure to come.

"We once had a 'Candid Camera' actor pose as a cat food manufacturer, asking a caterer to prepare a banquet for prize cats. The caterer never questioned the assignment. He planned a menu, starting with lobster bisque, and designed a centerpiece of celery for the cats to play with. He also suggested that the cats would enjoy a seating arrangement of male, female, male, and so on.

"When the caterer was informed he was on 'Candid Camera,' he laughed and gave us his permission to broadcast the segment. But as he was leaving, he stopped me and said, 'Now, about that banquet. I'll need at least four weeks' notice.'"

Again laughter swept through the audience.

The tone for the evening had been set earlier by Dr. Philip Zimbardo, head of the psychology department at Stanford University, who gave me an almost embarrassingly glowing introduction. He called me "one of our foremost natural social psychologists" who "spent his life creating little kinetic masterpieces on life-sized canvases that have drawn out of people some of the most vital aspects of human nature."

Phil concluded his introduction with a laudatory description of "Candid Camera" that left my head spinning. He said that the people photographed by "Candid Camera" were "challenged to cope, to endure, to find a way out, but to perform their assigned task, however bizarre, while retaining a quiet sense of dignity and human decency. And in the end, to maintain a sense of humor about the occasional foibles and little hassles that are a basic part of life. Unlike its current crop of weedy imitators, which make fun of people's pratfalls and pain, and seem to revel in their apparent stupidity, 'Candid Camera' lets us peek into the hearts and minds of Everyman and Everywoman. Doing so makes us all more humble, more worldly-wise, and perhaps even a bit more caring of one another."

I came to know Phil back in 1982 when he learned of my donation of the "Candid Camera" library to Cornell University and contacted us about using the clips in his classes at Stanford. The following year he arranged for me to speak at the 1983 Western Psychology Association convention; then, he came to my Pebble Beach house to interview me for an article in *Psychology Today* magazine.

Watching "Candid Camera," Phil had assumed that our gags were the result of special training I received in psychology. His first question in the interview was where I had earned my psychology degree. I told him I don't have such a degree. He then asked where I had taken classes in psychology. I told him I have never taken a psychology class in my life. When I told him I had never even read a book on psychology, he realized he had to throw out most of his prepared questions and take a different approach.

In the course of our conversation, Phil unearthed a fact about my past which I wasn't even aware of. I told him that while I was at Cornell, I had assisted in a study comparing the eating patterns of infants fed by nurses with those of infants fed by their mothers. I observed the subjects from behind a two-way mirror and recorded the results for the supervising professor.

When Phil asked this professor's name, I said, "He had just come over from Germany—Kurt something or other."

"Could it have been Kurt Lewin?" Phil asked, leaning forward.

"That was it. You know him?"

"Yes, of course. He's considered one of the most influential figures in our field—the founder of modern social psychology."

And now here I was, fifty-seven years after working for Professor Lewin, in an auditorium filled with 600 psychologists. I finished my speech and asked the audience for questions. A hand shot up. "Are there some negative traits in the human character which you've repeatedly seen surface as a result of your work?"

I often get variations of this question so I knew how to handle it. "The worst thing I see is how easily people can be led by any kind of authority figure, or even the most minimal signs of authority." I then described the "Delaware Closed Today" gag.

"We need to develop ways to teach our children how to resist unjust or ridiculous authority."

Another hand went up. "Can you tell us about some of the positive things you've learned about people from doing 'Candid Camera'?"

"Absolutely. Despite the way our society stresses conformity, I see many people striving to be unique from one another, creating something that is special about themselves. This individual variation makes people-watching so fascinating for me. I could enjoy watching people licking stamps and be repeatedly surprised by how they personalize this ordinary experience.

"But I must tell you that while we've learned much about people with 'Candid Camera,' I believe we could do more. I wish I could use our humorous and nonthreatening approach to help parents, teachers, or salespeople see their mistakes."

The audience was silent, then one more hand appeared. "What about you?" a woman asked. "How has making 'Candid Camera' helped you to live your life more productively or more happily?"

I paused. Usually, people aren't interested in me and my life. They want to hear about people caught by gags, how they respond, and what it means.

I answered slowly, feeling my way. "When a tragedy occurs, people often feel that the presence of humor is suddenly inappropriate. Their attitude seems to say, 'This is no laughing matter.' But I feel the opposite. I believe that laughing matters —and it's more essential for me in the tough times than ever."

After the speech ended, I thought how my views on the importance of laughter could have filled an entire lecture. I have come to believe that we learn through laughter and can even be healed by laughter.

These thoughts were not clearly formed as I stared through the two-way mirror at Cornell in 1934 or when I started "Candid Microphone" in 1947. But sometimes, looking back, I wonder if I wasn't intuitively guided by them. My first hard evidence that laughter was more than a pleasant diversion came in the sixties when Norman Cousins, then the editor of the *Saturday Review* contacted me and asked to borrow several "Candid Camera" shows.

Later I learned that Cousins had contracted an illness while traveling abroad. When he returned to the United States, his condition deteriorated to the point where it appeared he might die. Cousins discarded the advice of his doctors and took charge of his own treatment. By taking large doses of Vitamin C and watching "Candid Camera" tapes and Marx Brothers movies, he gradually recovered and lived productively for many years before dying from unrelated heart disease. He documented the enormous benefits of laughter in his book, *Anatomy of an Illness.*

Perhaps as a result of Cousins' book, I was contacted by Paul Newman who requested tapes for his friend John Huston, the great director, who was suffering from a very painful form of cancer. In a testimonial shot by my son Peter, Newman reported that every thirty minutes of watching "Candid Camera" gave Huston four pain-free hours. Years later, Newman called us again to borrow tapes for Mario Andretti's son, who was in great pain, recovering from injuries suffered in a car-racing accident.

These experiences along with my own reading on the subject made me think that while laughter clearly eases the suffering of pain, it might prove to have a healing effect as well. I wanted to establish a foundation to help others in pain and to collect more evidence in the form of actual patient testimonials.

The money for this foundation came from an unlikely source. As I mentioned in an earlier chapter, I was slandered by a former "Candid Camera" staff member who went on to become a popular talk show host. This woman, who must remained unnamed because of the terms of our settlement, claimed in her book that I exposed myself to her and the staff. Rather than suing her, as I'm sure she expected, I arranged to have her donate $25,000 to set up a foundation. I named that foundation Laughter Therapy. It seemed fitting that the money for this project should come as the result of such a laughable accusation.

Since Laughter Therapy was started in 1982, thousands of people have been involved in the program. We mail three hour-long tapes of "Candid Camera" scenes to people who are in pain from an illness or an accident. In selecting the sequences, I picked those that either get big laughs or have a life-affirming quality to them. In return, we ask that the person, or a representative, send us a letter describing the results.

Here's a letter from a woman in Oklahoma describing how the Laughter Therapy tapes helped her.

Even when I didn't feel like laughing and watching the Laughter Therapy tape, the person helping me out would put the VCR on and leave my bedroom to keep from being yelled at by me.

Since I would be confined to my bed during those times, and the TV and VCR are in my bedroom, there was nothing I could do about it but listen to the tape, even if I tried not to watch. Before long I'd end up watching and laughing about what I was seeing and not feeling any discomfort, and I don't think the exacerbation, or setback as I call it, lasted as long using the Laughter Therapy tape as without using it.

A popular piece on the Laughter Therapy tape is a gag in which a messenger was sent to deliver a package to an address in the Bronx. When the messenger got there, all he found was a door and doorbell—but no building. Still, he rang the bell and entered through the door, as if there was nothing odd about it.

A woman from Ontario, Canada, said this piece taught her a valuable lesson. "I now try to make conscious efforts to search for new ways to see and live, rather than just following 'standard procedures.' I stop more often now to appreciate the wonderful absurdities in life."

A woman from West Virginia said the Laughter Therapy tapes "definitely helped with depression and adjustment. With exercise, prayer, long walks, and your videos, I'm almost completely over the deep depression that I had. I viewed each several times, and it started me on the track to look for humor in everyday happenings—to pass on jokes and humorous stories. I deeply appreciate this service you have given me. Laughter is healing!"

In 1989, I had a firsthand opportunity to test my thoughts about laughter and healing. I had been having some chest discomfort and shortness of breath, but visits to various doctors in the preceding months had yielded nothing definitive. Then I happened to see a TV news report in which a Dr. Yuri Busi was describing his treatment of Lucille Ball, who had serious heart trouble. Among my fondest memories is the time I appeared as a guest in a "Lucy" show, and I listened intently as Dr. Busi explained how this lovely lady, only three years my senior, could still look forward to a productive life.

I decided to phone Dr. Busi and ask for an appointment. As I drove to his office the following day, the radio carried news that almost sent me into a ditch. Lucy was dead.

I managed to compose myself and continued on my way. A short while later, Dr. Busi was checking my blood pressure and probing my chest. Slowly, his expression clouded. This has to be one of the most frightening sights in the world. My imagination ran wild. After more tests, he told me I needed a heart bypass operation and arranged the earliest possible time for the surgery, which turned out to be a week later. As it was, he said I was running a high risk of having a heart attack at any time.

I went home, almost in tears. I'm a terrible coward, and when this kind of thing happens, I torture myself. In the midst of my panic, I recalled a story in the papers about how Carroll O'Connor, from "All in the Family," had recently undergone a similar bypass. I took the liberty of calling him.

It turned out that he was a fan of "Candid Camera," so we chatted about that for a few minutes. Then, I said, "Carroll, I just found out I have to have an operation like the one you went through. What's your advice?"

"When's the operation?" he asked.

"In a week."

He thought a moment, then said, "Now, I'm going to tell you what to do, and it's very important. Have the operation tomorrow."

This wasn't exactly what I wanted to hear. I couldn't hide my anxiety. "Why?"

"Because if you wait for a week, it'll be the worst week you ever live through."

"But I don't have a surgeon, I don't have a—"

"Get one and get it done!"

After I thanked him, I called Dr. Busi and told him what I wanted. Several hours later, he called back and said the only surgeon he could find on such short notice was a Dr. Taro Yokoyama who specialized in reconstructive heart surgery on infants. I decided that any doctor who could sew up tiny little hearts must be an incredible craftsman, so I agreed to have him do the bypass operation on me.

As I was prepped for the surgery, and chatted with Dr. Yokoyama, I found that he had an interest in Japanese gardens. I told him about the Japanese garden at my Nichols Canyon house, and he asked if he could come see it after the operation. His confident assumption that the operation would be a success gave me great hope. It also motivated me to make sure that we could walk through the garden together as soon as possible.

"What's the fastest you've ever discharged someone after a heart bypass?" I asked a nurse.

She looked at me quizzically, then answered, "We've had patients your age who left after only seven days."

I didn't say anything more, but I decided I was going to set a new hospital record.

The operation, and the delicate style of Dr. Yokoyama, made me feel as though someone from heaven came down to take care of me. When it was over, I felt great, and the scar on my chest is barely visible. The relief was enormous. I felt I was waking from a nightmare and beginning my life over again. I checked out of the hospital after six days.

I wanted to do something unusual to thank Dr. Yokoyama. I got a photograph of him and had his portrait done in a traditional form of Japanese stitchery. Then I had it framed and placed in a corner of the garden where Vladimir and I created a seating area, almost like a shrine, in his honor.

It was my intention to invite the doctor to visit this spot, to walk with me across the wooden bridge and up the pebbled path. I imagined us standing there, looking at his portrait and perhaps discussing how precious life is. But I could never bring myself to invite him. I had heard so much about his own fabulous garden that I felt embarrassed to show him mine. Perhaps if he reads this, he will know how truly grateful I am.

In the four years that have gone by since my operation, I've spent much time, alone, in that place in the garden. And I've gradually revised some of my thinking about what's important in life.

I decided to devote even more time to Laughter Therapy and to the educational and psychological applications of "Candid Camera." It was such thinking that brought me, in 1991, to the Western Psychological Association's convention and soon after that to a collaboration with Phil Zimbardo on a textbook and instructional video for college psychology courses. The venture, *Candid Camera Classics in Introductory and Social Psychology*, was published in 1993 by McGraw-Hill.

During my hours of thought in the garden, I've come to believe that there is a scale of happiness and sadness in every person's life. And that scale is precisely balanced. We never get more than a fifty-fifty break. The reason is, we don't understand one sensation without relating to its opposite. If we didn't know pain, we wouldn't know pleasure. If we didn't know poverty, we wouldn't appreciate riches.

Every experience only has meaning in terms of its opposite. I'm convinced of that. I also believe that you can live a life which is 98 percent joy, but then something in the last moments of your life could be so shattering as to bring you back to the balance point.

You can't beat the odds. Everything catches up with you.

Of course, I also cherish the notion that we all can benefit greatly by seeing ourselves as others see us. Which is to say, don't be surprised if sometime, somewhere, someplace when you least expect it...

But I hope you know the rest by now.

Epilogue

B Y   P E T E R   F U N T

On this particular Thursday, the daily twelve-noon call to my Connecticut office was right on time. It was nine a.m. in Hollywood, and my father's routine was to check in with me just after his West Coast office opened. Usually he'd want to talk about the work for the day, fine points of whatever deal we were negotiating, or some wild idea for a "Candid Camera" stunt that had popped into his head during a typically busy night of brainstorming.

But the voice on the other end of the phone was not my father's. His long-trusted gardener and jack-of-all-office-trades, Vladimir Rivera, was on the line and quite out of breath. He had arrived for work and discovered my father, semiconscious, on the floor. A short time later, doctors at Cedars-Sinai Medical Center confirmed that my father had suffered a severe stroke. It was soon clear that a new and exceedingly difficult chapter was about to be written in Allen Funt's life—a story he'd need help to tell.

231

It was a stroke that led to the death of his sister Dorothy when she was just sixty-two. "Some families have to worry about cancer, but we have circulatory weaknesses," my father once cautioned me. "Take good care of yourself."

But after his remarkable recovery four years earlier from heart bypass surgery, my father really hadn't been taking good care of himself. He was eating the wrong foods, skipping exercise sessions, and working long hours. In a way, his surgery had left him with a false sense of invincibility—as if he had become a bionic man.

To make matters worse, frustrations were mounting on the business front. The deal with the giant syndication company King World had produced an embarrassing flop. A home-video deal was foundering and yielding no profits. And a long-sought movie deal was proving elusive.

Then there was the strain of simply growing old. Some people handle this gracefully, but Allen Funt is not among them. He fights old age at every turn. When his hearing began to fail, for example, he refused to consider a hearing aid. Instead of getting a stronger prescription for his eyeglasses, he decided one day to stop wearing them altogether. Such instincts probably help extend his life; they certainly make it more exciting, but not without added tension and despair.

I had become much closer to my father in recent years after joining him as cohost, then host of our CBS specials. He was always supportive and spent years teaching me the tricks of a most unusual trade. But watching his son step into this role was an emotional challenge. Frequently he had to fight off the notion that perhaps "Candid Camera" should just fade out when it was time for him to step down.

I found myself reviewing so many of these emotional weights and measures when the doctor from the intensive care unit stepped out to give us his evaluation. My father's stroke had left him paralyzed on the right side, and his communication skills were seriously impacted. He had developed pneumonia while in the ICU and was in pretty rough shape.

Yet, even under such awful circumstances, my father's quirky good luck was with him. It turned out that his regular Los Angeles physician was announcing his retirement and couldn't handle the case. He recommended a cardiologist named Ray Weston. And so it was that this seventy-eight-year-old ICU patient came into the care of seventy-six-year-old Dr. Weston—an eccentric, crusty, yet extraordinary gent, who scolds the nurses, lectures the interns, and tirelessly inspires his patients to overcome the odds.

My father spent nearly five grueling months in the hospital. During that stretch Ray Weston never took a day off, never sent a "cover" doctor, and seemed to be there at all hours, especially when important decisions had to be made. Mostly, he used every bedside occasion to offer words of inspiration—not only to his patient, but to the staff and family who needed all the strength they could muster to think positively.

To avoid publicity during this ordeal, Allen Funt was listed on the hospital records as Len Fu. It is a pseudonym he has used many times, dating back to pre-Army days when he tried his hand as a writer of short stories. Frustrated by a string of rejections from magazines, my father decided to resubmit the manuscripts under a different name. It was his theory that an Asian-sounding name might have special appeal, so he fiddled with his own name and came up with Len Fu. It worked. Several of the stories were published, including one about a boxer who lay in a hospital, comatose, for many weeks. One day he was visited by a young fan, who had just learned to count. One, two, three, he began. At six the patient seemed to stir. At nine, he sat up! We told that story several times during the months at Cedars-Sinai.

Despite the false name, hundreds of letters and cards made it through to my father's hospital room. Most were from fans of "Candid Camera," some were from patients who had benefited from Laughter Therapy and wished to return the favor with a joke or funny story, and then there was this letter from Art Lee of Aurora, Illinois:

> You don't know me but I know of you.
>
> During 1944, as a member of the 42nd Infantry (Rainbow) Division, you brought many hours of good times to homesick GIs at Camp Gruber, Oklahoma. Your "Behind the Dog Tag" service club shows will never be forgotten.
>
> Your fellow Rainbow soldiers wish you a speedy recovery.

Mr. Lee's letter drew into focus the breadth of a fifty-year career devoted to entertaining people and helping them to smile.

On August 29, 1993, we chartered a plane to bring my father from Los Angeles to his home on the Monterey Peninsula to begin the rest of his life. Nowadays he's eating a perfect diet, exercising daily, and working with a speech therapist. Although confined to a wheelchair, he doesn't waste much time fretting.

Of course, he's retired from the business now, leaving it to me to carry on the "Candid Camera" tradition. He spends a lot of time with my two young kids, Stephanie and Danny, and my sister Patricia's daughter, Katie, and receives daily visits from Anne Flynn. Just before Thanksgiving he hosted a small dinner party for Dr. Weston and his wife Susan. It was a thankful time, indeed.

Since his stroke, many people have asked me about the role of Laughter Therapy in my father's own recovery. Fortunately, he isn't in great physical pain nor does he suffer from any disease. So in his case, the medical benefits of a hearty laugh are not clearly defined. Besides, having devoted most of his adult life to creating the "Candid Camera" library, he's not likely to be tickled by too many of its surprises.

Still, there are a few gems in our "Candid" collection that do provide him with therapeutic results. One sequence in particular, shot in 1976, features a six-year-old named Matt for whom fear and suffering were of no concern.

Allen: Do you believe in God?

Matt: Yes.

Allen: What does he look like?

Matt: I don't know what he looks like, but I know what my guardian angel looks like.

Allen: What does your guardian angel look like?

Matt: Well, she has wings.

Allen: Oh, did you ever see her?

Matt: No, you don't see a guardian angel. My mommy has a picture.

Allen: ...Of the guardian angel? You lucky son of a gun. Could I get a guardian angel? I don't think I have one.

Matt: You always have one.

Allen: Everybody has one? How do you find out who it is?

Matt: It's a lady, because I have a picture. It's true that you have a guardian angel, she's right close to you.

Allen: Did you ever get any help from your guardian angel? Did she ever protect you? Tell me one way so I'll believe it.

Matt: Well, I was going to get a cut when I tripped, you know. And I didn't get one.

Allen: I got a real cut. I almost broke my finger. What happened to my guardian angel there?

Matt: Well, she made it heal. You don't want it to stay that way.

Allen: Is your guardian angel helping you now?

Matt: She is.

Allen: All right, here's a job for your guardian angel. See this, I'm about to give you a punch right in the nose! Will your guardian angel help you?

Matt: Yes.

Allen: (His fist moves toward the boy's face.) Aren't you afraid?

Matt: No.

Allen: You *are* protected, aren't you?

Matt: Yes.

Allen: Give her my best regards, will you?

Matt: All right. I'll tell her.

Allen: How do you do it?

Matt: (His hands clasped.) You go like this, you look at your hands, and close your eyes, and think of what you're going to say to her.

Allen: What did you just tell her?

Matt: I love you.

As we watched that little boy on the screen, my father's face brightened. A knowing grin spread from his lips and puffed his cheeks.

Matt must be in his twenties now. Presumably he still has faith in his guardian angel. She does have special powers.

She gave us the first of what we hope will be our next million smiles.

Pebble Beach, California
February, 1994

ABC, 41, 52

Abeita, Jim, 182

Albert, Eddie, 65

Ali, Muhammad, 108-110, 162

Allen, Woody, 107, 109

Alma-Tadema, Sir Lawrence, 89-
90, 94-97, 109, 171

Andretti, Mario, 225

Ashley, Ted, 58, 147

Aubrey, James, 63

Ball, Lucille, 227

Banner, Bob, 58, 65, 67-68, 70

Baxter, Bob, 211-212

"Behind the Dog Tag," 25, 234

Berra, Yogi, 104

Bristol-Myers, 67

Burnett, Carol, 58, 106

Burns, Robert, 99

Busi, Dr. Yuri, 227

California Coastal Commission,
179

Camp Gruber, 25, 234

"Candid Kids," 7, 119, 121, 123,
125-127, 129, 174, 193-194

Cannon, Lester, 40, 135-136

Caputo, Rocky, 56, 178

Carson, Johnny, 64-65

CBS, 57-58, 63-65, 67, 69, 71, 74,
85, 99, 126, 133-134, 140, 142,
146, 164, 189-190, 192, 194-
195, 213, 232

Cedars-Sinai Medical Center, 231

Christman, Dick, 46, 75, 83, 204

Collins, Dorothy, 67-68, 207, 220

Conover Modeling Agency, 26

Cornell University, 16, 154, 222

Cousins, Norman, 224

Cox, Wally, 105

Crosby, Norm, 163

Curtis, Jamie Lee, 218

DeLuise, Dom, 198

Eastwood, Clint, 70

Eavesdropper at Large, 174

"Ed Sullivan Show, The," 63

"Facts of Life, The," 193

Farrow, Mia, 107

Faye, Joey, 110, 214

Flagg, Fannie, 102-103

Florman, Arthur, 75

Fox, Sonny, 42

Friedman, Ralph, 76

"Funny Money Man," 20

Garfield, John, 54

"Garry Moore Show, The," 57-58,
67, 111

George, Phyllis, 112

Gleason, Jackie, 56-57, 105

Gobel, George, 72

Godfrey, Arthur, 64-67, 69, 111-
112

Goldwater, Barry, 218

Grant, Arnold, 112

Green, Marge, 110

"Gripe Booth, The," 26

Grodin, Charles, 106

Hamburger, Philip, 53

Harby, Thorny, 183

Hargus, Dan, 211

Heberer, Nina, 42

Hery, George, 209

"Hidden Video," 189-192, 199, 201

Hirschfeld, Al, 21

Huston, John, 225

Jackson, Victoria, 111

Joelson, Ben, 110

Joslin, Elliot, 214

Kalb, Marvin, 140

Kaye, Danny, 120

Keaton, Buster, 105

King World, 198, 232

Kirby, Durwood, 111-112

Koch, Edward, 112

Krim, Arthur, 148

Kuperman, Howard, 76

Lamour, Dorothy, 105

Langeru, Giovanni, 32

Last Tango in Paris, 153

Laughter Therapy, 12, 226-227, 230, 234-235

Lee, Art, 234

Letterman, David, 218

Lever Brothers, 67

Lewin, Kurt, 223

Lewis, Richard, 218

Linkletter, Art, 120

Macy's, 18, 25

Maloney, John J., 36

Mansfield, Jayne, 104

Mantle, Mickey, 104

Marx, Harpo, 105

McGraw-Hill, 230

McKeon, Nancy, 193

Meadows, Audrey, 105

Metropolitan Museum, 96

Midnight Cowboy, 153

Money Talks, 7, 161-163, 165, 167-169, 171, 215

Moon, John, 179

Moore, Garry, 57-58, 67, 111

Morgan, Henry, 33

Morris, Jim, 195-196

Murray, Tom, 76

Mutual Broadcasting System, 26

"My Day," 19

Myerson, Bess, 112

NBC, 63, 193, 194, 205

Newman, Paul, 225

Nichols, Mike, 93

O'Connor, Carroll, 228

O'Malley, Tom, 110, 139

Odets, Clifford, 51

Odin, Curt, 18

Paar, Jack, 57, 205

Paley, Bill, 69, 142

Palmer, Betsy, 110

Parke Bernet, 94, 96-97, 171

Parton, Dolly, 104

Perlman, Itzhak, 93

Picker, David, 147-148

Pollard, Phil, 42

Redford, Robert, 217

Rich, Martin, 114
Richardson, Ann, 114
Richmond, Ray, 199
Rivera, Vladimir, 185, 231
Roberts, Ken, 52, 59
Roosevelt, Eleanor, 19
Routh, Jonathan, 193
Saroyan, William, 50-51
"Saturday Night Live," 111
Schwartz, Bob, 110, 213
Silvers, Phil, 104
Siskel, Gene, 155
Slep, Al, 42, 76, 79, 82, 99
Smile When You Say I Do, 172
Susskind, David, 50
Swayze, John Cameron, 59
"Tell it to the Camera," 192
Terzini, Pat, 114, 134
Tillman, Ray, 156

Truman, Harry, 91
United Artists, 147, 152-153, 161
Verne, David, 23
Warner Brothers, 147
WEAF, 20
Western Psychological
    Association, 220, 230
Weston, Dr. Ray, 233-234
*What Do You Say to a Naked
    Lady?*, 9, 146-157, 161, 187
"What's My Line?," 63
William Morris, 147
Winters, Jonathan, 106
Wrigley, Philip K., 19
Yokoyama, Dr. Taro, 228-229
"Your Hit Parade," 67
Zimbardo, Philip, 221
Zingale, Mike, 134, 139